BY SNOWSHOE, BUCKBOARD AND STEAMER

ALSO BY KATHRYN BRIDGE

Henry & Self
An English Gentlewoman at the Edge of Empire
Royal BC Museum, 2019

Emily Carr in England
Royal BC Museum, 2014

A Passion for Mountains
The Lives of Don and Phyllis Munday
Rocky Mountain Books, 2006

BY SNOWSHOE, BUCKBOARD AND STEAMER

WOMEN *of the* BRITISH COLUMBIA FRONTIER

KATHRYN BRIDGE

ROYAL **BC** MUSEUM

VICTORIA, CANADA

By Snowshoe, Buckboard and Steamer
Women of the British Columbia Frontier

First edition published by Sono Nis Press. Second edition published 2019
by the Royal BC Museum, 675 Belleville Street, Victoria, British Columbia,
V8W 9W2, Canada. Traditional territory of the Lekwungen (Songhees and
Xwsepsum Nations).

Cover by Lara Minja/Lime Design
Interior design and typesetting by Julie Cochrane
Index by Catherine Plear

LIBRARY AND ARCHIVES CANADA CATALOGUING IN PUBLICATION

Title: By snowshoe, buckboard and steamer : women of the British Columbia
    frontier / Kathryn Bridge.
Names: Bridge, Kathryn Anne, 1955- author. | Royal British Columbia
    Museum, publisher.
Description: Second edition. | Includes bibliographical references and index.
Identifiers: Canadiana (print) 20190096640 | Canadiana (ebook) 20190096683
    | ISBN 9780772673107 (softcover) | ISBN 9780772673114 (EPUB) | ISBN
    9780772673121 (Kindle) | ISBN 9780772673138 (PDF)
Subjects: LCSH: Women pioneers‚ÄîBritish Columbia,–Biography. | LCSH:
    Women travelers,–British Columbia,‚ÄîBiography. | LCSH: Frontier and
    pioneer life,–British Columbia. | LCSH: British Columbia,–Description and
    travel. | LCSH: British Columbia,–Biography. | LCGFT: Biographies.
Classification: LCC FC3817.2 . B74 2019 | DDC 971.1/020922,–dc23

10 9 8 7 6 5 4 3 2 1

Printed and bound in Canada by Friesens.

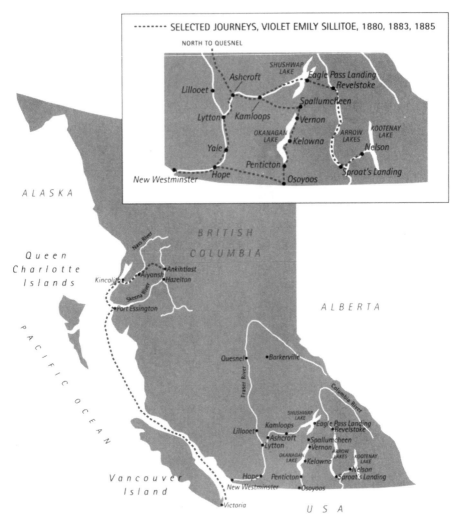

Introduction / 1

MARGARET ELIZA
FLORENCE ASKIN
agassiz
11

ELEANOR CAROLINE
fellows
43

HELEN KATE
woods
91

VIOLET EMILY
sillitoe
147

Sources / 198

Index / 202

ACKNOWLEDGEMENTS

Many people have provided assistance in locating photographs, making place-name identifications and confirming details. Thank you to Kelly Nolin and George Piercey of the B.C. Archives; Doreen Stephens, Anglican Diocese of New Westminster Archives; Ann Carroll, City of Vancouver Archives; Marnie Pickard, Agassiz-Harrison Museum; Dan Savard and Grant Keddie, Royal B.C. Museum; Simon Carey, England; Dorothy Dodge, Lytton; and Jim White of Ashcroft.

A special thank you also to the descendants of these frontier women who were interested and receptive when I telephoned and began asking questions about their grandmothers and great grandmothers: Anne Gray, Elizabeth Engle, Beth Van Blaricom, Ruth Longmate and Diana Brown. Ann West, former Sono Nis editor, was really the catalyst for this book. She would not let me rest after the publication of *Henry & Self,* urging me on, yet again. Diane Morriss, the book's first publisher, is to be congratulated for providing opportunities for books about B.C. women to become realities. Annie Weeks took my vague design ideas and made them a reality. Catherine Henderson, as always, shared my enthusiasm as I endlessly recounted "interesting tidbits" during the research phase. Kevin, Emma and Brendan Neary have co-operated in many ways to give me the time and space to write. Thank you all.

The list of thank-yous for this book must be updated, 21 years after its initial publication, to recognize Kelly-Ann Turkington of the Royal B.C. Museum, who arranged for images to be scanned, and to acknowledge the ongoing cooperation of the institutions and individuals who graciously allowed their images to be used. My thanks as well to the Royal B.C. Museum itself, for agreeing to publish this book.

Introduction

WHY?

Writers and historians tend to research what they would like to read. I like to read about women in the past and have a personal "need-to-know" fascination with the subject. It provides the stimulus for my delving. As the research progresses—clue piling upon clue—the fascination quickly becomes an addiction.

I am intrigued by the almost-undocumented hidden female strength of colonialism. I want to discover, and sometimes uncover, the life stories and personalities of nineteenth-century women—women who journeyed far from their birthplaces to begin new lives in the British colonies, in places like British Columbia, now a province of Canada, women who were strong in character and remarkable in their achievements.

The B.C. Archives is an irreplaceable repository of great historical wealth, and the information contained in the diaries, letters, manuscripts, journals, oral and published reminiscences, photographs, sketches and paintings collected and stored in this institution is of particular value. Each document provides clues to gather and build upon—little pieces of evidence that, when viewed together, flesh out the lives and circumstances of early settlers.

Only a small percentage of personal records have survived through time, and unfortunately, most of these historical documents were written by men. At times these records can provide information about women, but they do not contain the voices or perspectives of women. It is the quest for female voices that keeps me searching, focussed and energized.

It was in the records of the B.C. Archives that I encountered the four women of the frontier who are included in this volume. I found two of them while doing a history degree (one became the topic of a thesis). The other two were new discoveries made through a combination of deduction and serendipity as I searched through the manuscript indices at the archives, following every reference to documents written by women in a quest to find counterparts for the first two.

Although many references to immigrant women appear in the archives' collections, it is difficult to find enough information to enable a reconstruction of a life, or, more importantly, to present a woman as an individual, whose character, perspectives, worldviews or opinions emerge from the hidden clues contained in the documents. Not all immigrant women kept journals or wrote letters, nor were they all literate, and, unfortunately, not all the records have survived through time. What remains, therefore, provides information on a finite number of women, and only those who were literate. Despite these qualifiers, documents created by women provide important, balancing viewpoints for the times.

As a generalization, I found the most complete accounts were those written by women who might be described as middle-class, and my selection was made from among these. Their documents included letters, diaries, daybooks, household accounts, journals and reminiscences. I am aware that these four women represent only a portion of immigrant society. I wanted to include women from different walks of life, but I was limited by the availability of records as well as by the thoroughness of the documentation.

These women were also selected because their voices reflect different aspects of colonial history. Each of their accounts offers insight into the underpinning of relations between Indigenous and white people, relations among white people, and economic conditions, as well as communication and transportation activities.

They were all wives or daughters of upper-middle-class men, and their attitudes to their peers and others in society reflect an awareness of their station. They mixed socially with other immigrants of similar social standing, often developing lifelong friendships and alliances. These women were very secure in their sense of position within the social order and had, in their dealings with those they felt beneath them, a certain degree of arrogance born of their assumptions. Coupled with this white middle-class attitude of supremacy was a certain sense of awe and curiosity about the spectrum of life around them. The rawness and roughness of domestic life, housing, schooling and many other aspects of colonial living required flexibility, fortitude and a long-term outlook. All had to make adjustments, whether because of the requirements of physical labour, forced reliance on neighbours for assistance, the lack of cultural standards and entertainments, or interaction with the Indigenous population. Sometimes the most radical contrasts from old to new were fondly recalled later, in direct contrast to the daily reality, which had been undoubtedly stressful.

Despite these commonalities, there are differences between the women and in their accounts. Their adventures take place from the 1860s to the 1890s and occur in geographically disparate parts of British Columbia, ranging from the Fraser Valley to the Nass and Skeena Rivers, and from Victoria to the Cariboo, Okanagan and Kootenays. The company they kept was different, whether strictly within a peer group or cautiously explorative outside their set. Relationships between the women and their husbands ranged from indifference to true companionship.

Each woman was, in her own way, on the frontier. This frontier was a personal rather than geographic one, although the challenges of travel imposed by distance and landscape in some ways make us link the concepts.

The wild west, prairie acres, wagon trains and skirmishes with Indigenous peoples—this is a generalized American perspective of frontier. Some historians argue that Canada did not have a frontier; they claim that the Canadian west developed differently than the west in the United States.[1] And so it has. But frontiers can also describe situations or circumstances in which events occur that are on the edge or in advance of what follows. This linking of people, and particularly individuals, to a frontier of opportunity is precisely what I had in mind when writing this book. I wanted to present the circumstances of immigrant women in nineteenth-century British Columbia who had, for one reason or another, moved from another country to this area, and whose lives were consequently altered by their extraction from homelands and by the necessity to adapt to a new and different life. These women were—to borrow from the other frontier definition—trailblazers. They were on the edge; they had opportunities unheard of in their home countries—opportunities that would not be available decades later. This was a unique transition from old world to new world as social patterns and conventions were disrupted and the status quo dissolved. The very newness of the land for these women and the informality of authority and regulations made it possible for them to break away from some stereotypical molds.

THE SETTING

The area we now call British Columbia was, until the mid-nineteenth century, a landscape populated by First Nations who lived off the land and sea. Apart from a brief Spanish occupation at Yuquot (Friendly Cove, Nootka Sound) in 1792–3, no immigrant settlements existed until the Northwest Company established its first outposts: Fort Kamloops on the Thompson River in 1812 and Fort Alexandria on the Fraser in 1821. Soon a network of Hudson's Bay Company outposts was established along major rivers, and overland trails brought traders into close contact with Indigenous people who traded furs, fish, grease and other products for European food staples such as sugar and flour as well as blankets, beads, axes and other tools. In 1843 Fort Victoria on Vancouver Island was built as the Pacific headquarters for the Hudson's Bay Company's trade west of the Rocky Mountains. It developed slowly. In 1854, the immigrant population around the fort stood at 232, and the area boasted 79 dwelling houses, 12 stores and shops, one church and one school.[2]

The Fraser River gold rush of 1858 and the Cariboo gold rush of 1862 brought tens of thousands of men into Fort Victoria, initially for provisioning and later for shelter during the winter months. The population grew literally overnight, and while most of the unsuccessful miners left the colonies after the rushes, a certain percentage stayed on. By 1862 the population was estimated at 6,000, and the community comprised 1,500 buildings. The population levelled off to about 4,600 in 1874,[3] and the 1881 census enumerated 4,453 white people, 583 Chinese people, and 192 Indigenous people.

The frontier women entered a world where they were a clear minority. The white settlements were populated primarily by men. Many of these men had worked for the Hudson's Bay Company and lived a life where few white women appeared. The male-to-female ratio amongst immigrants was a staggering 100:1 in 1865,[4] improving to 3:2 by 1881.[5] The lack of immigrant women in the colonial period was a situation of great concern to the government and to the residents, for the premise of colonial development was founded on the assumption of families and stability. With small numbers of women, the incentive for immigrants to remain was not strong, and without domestics, those few women already resident had a hard life indeed. The situation was acknowledged in England, and in September 1862 the first "bride ship", the *Tynemouth*, arrived in Esquimalt Harbour and unloaded its cargo of 60 unmarried women.

As the numbers of immigrants from Great Britain increased, the local social structure mimicked that of British society. Society was viewed as a series of strata defined by purely British expectations and standards. Thus an upper class of landed Hudson's Bay Company officials and their families presided over the families of numerous middle-class professionals, shopkeepers and businessmen. Next were the labouring classes and finally, the non-British, non-Europeans—the Hawaiian, Black, Chinese and Indigenous people. However, the colonial immigrant population was very cosmopolitan, and this hierarchy was in flux. As one scholar noted, it was "an amazingly complex group of peoples claiming an equally amazing variety of nations as their homeland."[6] Living in the colony often forced immigrants to make adjustments. They were distanced from the social conventions, politics and alliances of their home countries, away from family, friends and authority. Some frontier women took advantage of these conditions and did not adhere rigidly to convention. Others saw only the restrictions imposed by their lack of numbers.

The immigrants held particular world views. For British immigrants, this meant a belief in the importance and even superiority of English society and the British Empire, an empire that stretched out to far-flung corners of the globe. The colonies "claimed" by Great Britain were for the use of her citizens—available for settlement, exploitation and profit. The immigrants, therefore, viewed the new lands and peoples with "Imperial

Eyes."[7] This meant viewing Indigenous people as a "conquered race," useful for cheap labour, needful of conversion to Christianity and, in many cases, suitable for ignoring altogether.

It has been estimated that the pre-contact population of British Columbia was 300,000.[8] By 1830, because of the ravages of smallpox and other diseases introduced by explorers and traders, it was no more than one-eighth this number. By 1881, the time of the first Canadian census for the province, subsequent epidemics had further reduced the First Nations population to approximately 29,000.[9] By the time colonists and miners arrived in the 1850s and 1860s, the landscape had been severely depopulated. What appeared to the new arrivals as "a vast wilderness," principally uninhabited, had been until the previous 50 years or so a richly populated and utilized landscape. Despite the decimation of their numbers, Indigenous people were very visible in and around the immigrant settlements, and they greatly outnumbered the newcomers for many decades.

For many it was an unsettling experience to arrive in these distant lands and find oneself directly confronted with a highly visible "conquered" race. This sense of vulnerability was experienced doubly by the frontier women, because they also entered a predominantly male society, set, as they saw it, within a wilderness populated by an Indigenous population many times their number.

Being part of a minority group was a new reality for most white women. Some retreated into the social conventions they had been brought up in and interacted as little as possible with the First Nations, barely acknowledging their existence. Others expressed curiosity, albeit mixed with an ethnocentric bias. A few used the situation as an opportunity to develop personally by overcoming their preconceived notions and taking the time and care to interact with individual Indigenous people on a personal basis.

The landscape was a geographical frontier, since it was a great unknown, largely untrodden by immigrants although known intimately by Indigenous people. As the newcomers moved away from the havens of Victoria and New Westminster into "the wilderness," how did they react to travelling through vast areas unpopulated by fellow immigrants? How did the women deal with the physical discomfort of travel by canoe, horseback or buckboard? Some women refused to extend themselves beyond the safe cocoons of immigrant settlements; others masked their fear, followed their husbands and adapted by necessity; still others undertook journeys in a spirit of adventure.

The women recorded their days in diary entries and wrote home, relating news, describing adventures and keeping their families informed. The families cherished these letters and in many cases preserved them for future generations. The women were aware that their experiences were unprecedented, presenting sharp contrast to their previous activities. In some cases, as these frontier women aged and reflected back on their lifetimes, they realized that their experiences of British Columbia during those early days had lasting interest, as the province had changed greatly. The incredible increase in the immigrant population and advances in technology, communication and travel had created urban centres and changed forever the frontier as they had lived it. So significant was the contrast that some of these women decided to write about their own life experiences as a means of documenting bygone times. Two of the four women in this volume wrote reminiscences that were self-published; the third had her account published posthumously.

In studying these women, one characteristic is definitely communicated across the years. It is their excitement and the zest for life. In some cases it leaps out at you from the pages, while in others it is quietly understated. From the perspective of the late twentieth century, it makes for captivating reading.

THE WOMEN

The four women whose lives are included in this volume left accounts of travelling to the west and also of their explorations and excursions in British Columbia. Their writings unveil their emotions at the time and give details of living conditions, discomforts and adventures along the way. Some document the women's awareness of their own changing attitudes toward the environment, Indigenous people and colonial living generally. Others offer detailed accounts of daily life, chronicle journeys and record the conversations and opinions of their peers and acquaintances. These latter accounts hold a wealth of historical evidence for re-creating the times. I rely primarily on the women's own words to tell their stories, but I have provided biographical sketches as a frame for sections of their writings. This context makes the personalized accounts understandable in relation to the lives and times of the women. Notes following each chapter expand on the major figures and events recorded in the accounts. Two of the women were talented amateur artists whose pencil sketches and watercolour paintings document their activities and surroundings. I have included many of these art works alongside the writings to supply additional information and to show how the women used art to augment their written descriptions.

Eleanor Fellows was an avid letter writer and a published author of numerous articles on subjects ranging from the Penny Post to Shakespeare, Chaucer and Milton. In her 80s she self-published her *Reminiscences*, which included several chapters about her life in British Columbia during her short residence there from 1862 to 1866. Her accounts included here were written many years later; however, the details and anecdotal information make them important records of early social life in Victoria. Her stories provide documentation of a pivotal time after the gold rushes, when the fort was evolving into a town and a permanent, non-fur-trading population was forming, and of a time when Vancouver Island was a British colony, separate and distinct from the mainland.

Violet Sillitoe lived until the age of 78, and outlived her husband by 40 years. She was deeply aware of the importance of the observations she made when, as a young bride, she accompanied her husband, the first Bishop of New Westminster, on trips throughout the province. Her observations were originally recorded in letters to her mother. Violet later used these letters to write two small self-published volumes of reminiscences that record her travel around the province, through the Okanagan and Fraser Canyon and in various mining communities. Her accounts of travelling were also included in various Anglican Church publications as a means of informing church benefactors and supporters about vital missionary work.[10] In her travels she met many people, and she recorded these encounters in her letters, preserving dialogue and using vivid imagery to re-animate the accounts with immediacy and great readability. Her description of a royal visit is a jewel.

Helen Kate Woods' account of her overland snowshoe journey provides a unique window into winter travel and gives a thorough impression of how isolated settlers became when the snows arrived. She kept a journal en route to record the details of each day's experiences. As such, the account is sometimes rough, without the polish of the published reminiscences of Eleanor Fellows, Violet Sillitoe or Florence Agassiz, but its strength and emotional appeal lies in its immediacy. It has not been re-written or coloured by the passing of years or later reflection. The account has been transcribed here in its entirety.

Florence Agassiz came to the colonies as a child and lived at Hope and Yale before settling in the Fraser Valley. Her account recalls these early years from an adult's perspective. Agassiz's story is preserved because her children insisted that she write it down. In the preface to her *Memories of Pioneer Life in British Columbia*, Agassiz writes, "My children are anxious to have me write a history of my family and their pioneer days in British Columbia, so I have promised to do my best, although I have told them that I am afraid they will be disappointed at the lack of wild adventure there."[11]

It is my hope that readers of this volume will find the "wild adventure," place themselves in the positions of these frontier women and relive their moments in British Columbia's past.

NOTES

1 Frederick Jackson Turner, an American historian, postulated a "frontier thesis" to explain the westward development of his country. Over the decades, great debate and much historical discourse surrounding his concepts resulted in new, revisionist historical study. In Canada, historian J.M.C. Careless offered his own "metropolitan thesis" as a counter to Turner's thesis, arguing different reasons for Canada's unique development. This theory also has been greatly debated and spawned other successive interpretations, which continue to be discussed.

2 Typescript, vertical file, B.C. Archives, n.d.

3 Ibid.

4 Matthew Macfie, *Vancouver Island and British Columbia* (London: Longman, Green, 1865), p. 406.

5 Quoted in Cole Harris, *The Resettlement of British Columbia* (Vancouver: University of British Columbia Press, 1997), p. 138.

6 Frederick E. Walden, "Social History of Victoria, British Columbia, 1858–1871," essay for bachelor's degree, University of British Columbia, 1951, p. 1.

7 Mary Louise Pratt, *Imperial Eyes* (London: Routlege, Chapman and Hall, 1992).

8 Cole Harris, *The Resettlement of British Columbia* (Vancouver: University of British Columbia Press, 1997), p. 138.

9 Ibid., p. 294.

10 *Columbia Mission Annual Reports* included submissions by clergy "in the field," as did *Mission Life*, both published in London, England.

11 Florence Goodfellow, *Memories of Pioneer Life in British Columbia* (Vancouver: Kent Centennial Committee), p. 5.

MARGARET ELIZA
FLORENCE ASKIN

agassiz

1854–1940

Florence at 24 with her first child, 1878. B.C. ARCHIVES G-8478.

MARGARET ELIZA FLORENCE ASKIN AGASSIZ was born in London, Canada West (later Ontario), on 23 September 1854. She was the second child of Lewis Nunn Agassiz and his wife, Mary Caroline (née Schram). Florence, as the girl was known, lived in British Columbia at a time of great change, witnessing first-hand the effects of the Cariboo Gold Rush, which brought so many thousands through the Fraser Valley and up-river. Her family lived at Yale and Hope, finally establishing a farm in the Fraser Valley. They were isolated from other white settlements and dependent upon the river and sloughs for transportation by boat, as roads were non-existent and the railway decades away. Florence was a child who adapted quickly to the new ways of colonial life; as an adult she remembered the fun and excitement of her lifestyle and circumstances rather than the negativity of hardship, isolation and lack of "advantages." In her 70s she was persuaded by her family to write the story of her life, which she titled *Memories of Pioneer Life in British Columbia*. This account was later published as a small booklet in 1941 and reprinted by the Kent Centennial Committee during the B.C. Centennial celebrations in 1958. At the outset of her *Memories*, Florence modestly states that she is afraid the reader "will be disappointed at the lack of wild adventure there."[1]

Although she may not have recognized it, her life did contain "wild adventures." To give her voice precedence over mine, I have quoted extensively from *Memories* to tell Florence's story. With a lifetime's perspective, Florence wrote simply and tended to underplay the drama of certain events, rarely breaking her narrative stride. She also placed herself in the role of a narrator, distancing herself from the events. Reading her account today, in a much-changed world where highways and planes make travel in the province quicker and less than a hardship, we have the

Florence Agassiz and her siblings just prior to their voyage out to British Columbia, 1861. L TO R: Jane Vandine Caroline Agassiz; Lewis Arthur Agassiz; Margaret Eliza Florence Askin Agassiz; James Burwell Agassiz.

PHOTOGRAPHER: J. EGAN'S PORTRAIT GALLERY, LONDON, ONTARIO. B.C. ARCHIVES G-7214.

perspective of technological change, which allows us to appreciate how different, demanding and challenging life must have been for Florence Agassiz.

Florence was just seven years old when she, her elder brother, Arthur, her mother, and her two younger siblings, Jane and James, arrived in Esquimalt Harbour on the *Oregon* in April 1862. It had been a long, eventful voyage, complicated by a series of childhood illnesses. There to meet them was Florence's father, Lewis Nunn Agassiz, former Captain in the Royal Welsh Fusiliers. They had been separated for over three years.

Agassiz seems to have been a bit of a rover, chasing one dream and then another.[2] He left his family in Canada West in 1858, boarding the steamer *Brother Jonathan* bound for California via Cape Horn. He stopped for a time in California, then came north to the colony of British Columbia, seeking his fortune in the rush for gold. Agassiz mined along the Fraser River as far as Lytton and later ventured to Quesnel and, finally, William's Creek. He was largely unsuccessful. Wintering over in Victoria in the fall of 1861, Agassiz took the advice of Governor James Douglas,[3] who pointed out to him something that he probably already knew: valuable farmland in the Cariboo district had greater potential for a family man than did the backbreaking life of a gold miner.[4] Wasting no time, Agassiz wrote to his wife, Caroline, suggesting that a good life could be made in cattle ranching. Specifically he fancied the Williams Lake area, where huge tracts of good land could be pre-empted at very little cost. Caroline and their four children booked passage on a steamer and joined him the following April. Florence later recalled:

So in March 1862 we left London, Canada West, for New York, much against the wishes of our grandparents whom we children never saw again…. In New York we children all came down with mumps at the hotel and had to stay there a week before taking a boat for the Isthmus of Panama. My mother had offered to pay half the expenses of a young girl who was going to Victoria to be married if she would help her with the children en route, but being ill all the way, she was far more trouble than she was worth. My mother was very much annoyed by a lot of Federal officers on board, who were always talking about what they would do to the South. Mother said she hoped most ardently that the *Alabama* would happen along and capture them all, a thing which actually happened on the boat's next trip.

We were cautioned against eating fruit at the Isthmus, as it was considered almost a death spot, so many people died when making the journey. (During the building of the railway they said the roadbed could have been paved with the bodies of the poor men who died.) We took only a pineapple and a coconut on board the boat for San Francisco.

There was a man on that boat to whom for some reason, I took a great dislike. Mama thought him very entertaining, but he was too funny for my taste, and when, a few days out, Arthur brought the coconut out to be eaten, he capered around and clapped his hands, to my mind in a most undignified manner. When the coconut was cracked open, instead of luscious meat and milk there was only an enormous spider in a web. I couldn't help giving him a most vindictive look.

We landed without mishap at Aspinwall (renamed Colon), and spent the night there, crossing by railway to Panama the next day. While in the harbour we children got much joy by dropping pennies into the water for the natives to dive after. We took ship again (an old side-wheel steamer), calling at Acapulco on the way up the coast and arrived without accident at San Francisco. Here mother met an old friend who had lost her eldest son while crossing the Isthmus and she was suffering terribly from homesickness.

We were forced to wait one week here before we could get a boat for Vancouver Island. The old Lick House was then in course of construction—for many years the best hotel on the coast and always spoken of by Californians with great pride.

A week after leaving San Francisco, we arrived in Esquimalt with the measles. We were told afterward that all children sailing on the *Oregon* got the measles. They could not have known very much about disinfecting in those days. We recovered rapidly, however. Father met us at Esquimalt where the boat docked, with an express wagon, into which he piled all of our luggage, and to our great joy, we three eldest on top. He, Mother and little brother James (whose fourth birthday it was), sat in front as we drove the five miles into Victoria where we took a cottage for a month, and our parents saw our lady companion safely married to her happy young carpenter.

Preparations had to be made and our plans laid for the trip into the

Cariboo, where Father intended to locate. The only furniture in the cottage was a small cooking stove, a bedstead, a deal table and boxes for chairs. We children thought it was great fun. We had been there only a few days when a band of camels arrived and were penned in a large field at the back of the house.[5] Needless to say, we children spent most of the time on top of the high board fence surrounding them, it being the first time we had ever seen a camel. They were intended for pack animals in the northern plains of British Columbia, but [they] frightened the horses so badly it was impossible to use them. The climate did not agree with them and they all died off after a while except one tough old fellow who lingered on for a number of years wandering around the settlement of Kamloops. I have always thought the town was named after them and is not an old Indian name as most people seem to think, having forgotten all about the poor old camels.

In Victoria, we bought two horses and a mule and all the supplies considered necessary for the journey. Arthur, my eldest brother, aged nine, had to take the animals to a grassy spot and herd them *every* day. He took little James, aged four, for companionship (the poor children had never been anywhere without a nurse, before), and would leave him to watch the horses while Arthur went to the beach and caught crabs. One day, James and the horses all disappeared. Arthur ran home in terror to find James had been found in tears by a clergyman and taken home, but the horses had wandered off and some time was spent in recovering them.

From Victoria we crossed to New Westminster on the mainland by means of a small steamer, the *Otter*, a side-wheeler. A friend of my father's, a Mr. Finlaison,[6] head of the Government customs, met us and insisted that we stay with him during the week we had to wait for another boat to take us up the Fraser. Mr. Finlaison and my father had built a hotel in [New] Westminster some time before, but it had burned down and they lost all they had put into it. It was our intention to take the steamer *Yale*, but that ill-fated craft had blown up on its last trip in an attempt to put on enough steam to make the rapids just below the little settlement of the same name, and its master, Captain Jamison,[7] was killed.

Mr. Finlaison was a bachelor and had a nice little house and garden. He later married a daughter of one of the engineers and had a family of eleven sons and finished with twin daughters.

We children enjoyed our visit very much, even though we were frightened every evening when the chain gang passed, and it was here also we had our first experience with mosquitoes.

After a few days the steamer *Hope* arrived to take the place of the *Yale* and we all embarked for the trip up the mighty Fraser river, which at this time of year was in flood and very dangerous. The steamers had to burn wood as they had not discovered the coal deposits yet, so they had to stop and take on wood at different places, the Indians carrying it to the boat on their backs.

We reached the Harrison, a very beautiful tributary to the Fraser late the same afternoon. While the boat was unloading local freight, my father went on shore and cut wild grass for the horses, which he tied into bundles and he and little Arthur carried it aboard the boat. The steamer went on up the river to the lake of the same name, where the now noted hot springs are located, and from there up the lake to Douglas, at that time the best route to the Cariboo. After discharging freight, we retraced our way to the Fraser and continued up that river until we came to Emory's Bar. Here, after several attempts to make the rapids, Captain Ainsley (commonly known as Delaware) decided it was useless and landed the passengers and freight on the bank. From this point to our destination, Yale, was only five miles, but over a mountain trail which had not been used for a year. All the old campaigners packed up and went on that evening, but my father thought it better for us to camp there for the night.

After putting up the tents and taking care of the horses, he showed mother how to cook dinner over a camp fire. Dinner over and the children in bed, father and mother went to the bank of the river where mother was given a lesson in panning gold. While they were enjoying themselves, two Indians appeared, and seeing the tents, poked their heads through the opening which frightened us nearly out of our senses. Our screams terrified the Indians and also our parents, who came running to the scene. It took some time to pacify us, but at last all was still and we slept soundly through our first night in the forest. We found later, however, that during the night an Indian dog had made off with a ham worth in those days about twenty dollars.

The next morning on waking we were thrilled to see across the river the wreck of the steamer *Yale*.

We had two horses and a mule. My mother with the youngest boy in her arms was mounted, then innumerable bundles were tied on all sides. Large pack-saddles were put on the other horse and the mule, to which sacks of flour, sides of bacon, bags of beans, and it seemed to me, every imaginable thing was fastened. On top of the mule's load were put my little sister, Jinny, aged five, and me, aged seven. My father then shouldered a large pack himself, and with Arthur leading the other horse, we started over the next to impossible trail. As I said before, it had not been used for a year until the other passengers from the boat had gone over it. There were innumerable fallen trees across the path which caused the horses to fall. Mother's horse fell backwards several times, throwing her and my small brother off and scattering bundles in all directions, and my poor little sister, Jinny, was continually sliding from the back of the mule, and Father was always rushing up to replace people and baggage. To cap the climax, the horse Arthur was leading stepped on his foot and hurt him badly. It is a wonder to me that we all got through alive.

It was dark night when we arrived at the log cabin on the outskirts of Yale, a very tired and discouraged family. The only furniture was a stove and several bunks built one above the other on the side of the wall. By lantern light we got something to eat and were put to bed. I have often heard my mother say that notwithstanding the terrible outlook of danger, hardship and drudgery, that when she opened the door of the little log cabin the next morning and saw the glorious panorama of mountain, vale and river, such a feeling of joy and exultation flowed through her, it seemed to sweep away every doubt and dread. As for the children, well, we were beside ourselves with joy. The rarefied mountain air was so exhilarating, we raced up and down the mountainside, found beautiful flowers, caught fish in a leaping, sparkling stream, and only wished to live on there forever.

That afternoon we all walked into the little mining town of Yale. It must have been a curious sight for those poor hardworking miners to see a refined and dainty little lady with four nicely dressed little children walking through the one sordid street. They all came to their doors and watched us pass. The new Cariboo road had just been commenced. A regiment of engineers, sappers and miners had been sent from England to build it and any other much needed road. We walked through Yale to where the road began. Only about half a mile was finished, cut out of solid rock, sheer mountain above and sheer precipice down to the boiling Fraser below. Beyond this was the old trail looking like a scratch, winding in and out among the mountain. Poor Mother looked at it. "Is that the road we have to travel to reach the promised land?" she asked. Father said, "It is not so bad as it looks." "I would rather go back to Victoria and take in washing," she said.[8]

That was the end of Cariboo dreams. Florence's mother, a woman of considerable character and fortitude, due in part to her United Empire Loyalist background,[9] had made a decision. The thought of maneuvering four youngsters and overpacked animals along a narrow strip of roadway above the rushing Fraser River convinced her. She would take the situation as she knew it rather than risk the unknown. In the long run, this was probably the wisest thing to do. The realities of travel along the Cariboo Wagon Road, so equipped, would have daunted a more experienced traveller. Florence recalled what came next:

> We turned and walked back. Then Mother asked him who was the highest official in town. He said a Stipendiary Magistrate, Saunders[10] by name, so they called on him, told him all about it and asked if there was any position he could give my father. Mr. Saunders was a very charming man, an Englishman by birth. He had been an officer in the Austrian army. He said we had come in the nick of time as there was a position open as Chief Constable and postmaster at Hope, a few miles down the river. It had been the head of navigation until the government started to build the road at Yale a few months before. Of course this position was accepted with joy, although the salary was very small. We had a small remittance from England every year and a house and large garden went with the position. We sold one horse and the mule, taking the other horse with us.
>
> The steamer was leaving the next day, so we again put all our belongings on board and were not long in reaching Hope as the river was running very swiftly.
>
> Mother was very pleased to find that there were many fine women in the small community. The Rev. Mr. Pringle,[11] of the Church of England,[12] with his wife, and four little girls just our ages, had a very

pretty church which everyone attended. The Hudson's Bay Company's factor, Mr. William Charles,[13] was there with his wife and family. Mr. Landvoight[14] with a nice little French wife, owned the principal store. A family named Glennie[15] had a small farm close to town. The office of Chief Constable, which my father accepted, was the only official position representing the government and carried with it the position of postmaster, mine recorder, licences, etc.

The house was quite comfortable, consisting of a very large office across the front and a large living room, two bedrooms and a kitchen…. Hope was a most exciting and thrilling place for children in those days. All through the spring and summer months, long pack trains were coming and going into the Kootenay Country.[16] We used to watch them being packed—such rearing, kicking, bucking and chucking of packs. There were hundreds of Chinamen going into the goldfields carrying their own supplies. They would follow one another in single file, their packs on each end of a pole carried over their shoulders—large mat sacks filled with rice, tea, dried fish, etc. They always went along at a jog trot; we had never seen anything to compare with it before. The Chinamen were very fond of mining. We could see them all up and down the river on the sand bars, working with pans and rockers.

The Indians liked to look through the windows at night into our lighted rooms, at first frightening us very much, but we soon got used to them and became very friendly and learned very quickly to speak the Chinook jargon so that we could converse with them with ease. In winter the Indians all went to live in what they called Keekwillie holes, a large, deep, round hole in the ground, covered by a large roof topped with branches of trees interwoven with a layer of clay and earth on top, making an immense mound. Here the whole tribe lived all winter. They had an open fire in the centre and a hole in the roof through which both the smoke and the Indians had exit….

The families were all very congenial. There was no school but my dear mother taught us very faithfully. She herself had a hard time learning to cook. I remember her weeping bitterly with a batch of bread burned to a cinder on the floor in front of her, but she soon overcame these difficulties and became an expert in the culinary art. We could always get Indian women to do the washing and scrubbing….

Two of my sisters, Minnie and Connie, were born in Hope. My poor mother who had never been confined without a doctor, was quite sure she would never live through the ordeal. She was able to get a clever experienced nurse from [New] Westminster and came through very well in spite of the fact that she had been considered a very delicate woman.

Poor Mrs. Pringle had had two children in Hope and was expecting another. There was some misunderstanding about the nurse, for the baby came before she did, and poor mother (who had never seen a confinement before) had to take care of her. With Mr. Pringle calling directions from a doctor's book outside the door, however, all went well and the baby was the longed-for little boy.

After two and a half years Mr. Commeline, who was Chief Constable and postmaster at Yale, decided to give up his position and go home to England and my father was promoted, so we were all shipped back to Yale, which was now the head of navigation. The Cariboo road was finished. Thousands of people and tons of freight now went through on stage and wagons. To pay for the road and maintenance, the government put in a toll gate and weighing station....

We did not like Yale as well as we did Hope. Most of the trees had been cut down, and the town was built on the side of a mountain. The sun poured down on the rocky slope making it very hot, and in winter it was correspondingly cold. We used to get a lot of fun coasting down the side of the mountain and out onto the frozen snow on the level for a long distance, sometimes hitting a hidden rock and upsetting. None of the other children in the town had ever tried this form of amusement, but we soon coaxed a little girl named Harriet Oppenheimer,[17] to go with us, but unfortunately we hit a rock the first time we went down and took a terrible spill, and poor lovely little Harriet's face was badly skinned. We rushed her into Mama for first aid, who applied a healing lotion. It did not take long to heal, but neither she nor any other of the children would trust themselves to our tender mercies on the mountainside again.

Mr. Joseph Trutch[18] and his brother, John, civil engineers, were building a suspension bridge across the Fraser a few miles from Yale. It was considered a wonderful piece of engineering work and was called the Alexandria [sic] bridge[19]....

My mother wished very much to go for a drive up the Cariboo road to see the suspension bridge, and the brewer offered my father his horse and spring wagon; so we had a delicious lunch packed in a champagne basket, (champagne baskets were plentiful and put to many uses) and we all got in the wagon. The horse trotted along beautifully through the town, and we all sat up feeling very pleased with ourselves, when a lot of little children ran out shouting, "Smarty boots, proudy hoops" after us. We were very thankful they did not see our ignominious return. After we passed the tollgate we came to rather a steep hill which the horse absolutely refused to climb. Father tried every known trick to start a balky horse, but he stood perfectly still. After standing for about half an hour he suddenly started on his own, and he went through the same performance every hill we came to, and there were many hills.

About 2 p.m. we reached a roadhouse called "the Frenchman's,"[20] about five miles out of town. Our parents decided that it was too late to go further, so we had our picnic on a grassy shelf overhanging the river. Father went to get the horse which he had stabled at the Frenchman's, and that good man started to put the harness on him. The brute of an animal let out at him with both hind legs, sending him flying. Frenchy clasped himself around the middle, yelling, "Oh, my bellee, my bellee." Father rushed over to him and picked him up, took him into the bar and gave him a couple of stiff drinks. In a few minutes he was all right again. Father told Mama to take us down the road, while he was hitching the horse to the wagon, and said he would pick us up shortly. We walked on and on, Mama carrying the baby. The sky became overcast and the rain came down in torrents. When we had gone about two miles Father and Arthur caught up with us, but that brute of a horse had decided to stay at the Frenchman's. He had behaved like a mad thing, thrashing out with his legs, and wouldn't let anyone come near him. Father, thinking that he would probably kick the wagon to pieces even if he got him hitched, decided to leave him there all night and let his master get him in the morning. He picked up little Connie, and we all trudged along in the soaking rain until we came to the toll-gate. The gate-keeper and his wife were very kind and took us in. The bright, cheerful fire warmed and dried us. There were a number of delicious looking pies standing on the table which I am afraid we children eyed hungrily, for the kind woman gave us each a large piece. Dried and rested we started off again in the dark and in a little while arrived home….

The people of Yale often had dances, but none of the ladies on the hill above the town had ever attended them. It had never occurred to them that the people would be offended, until a delegation from the town called on them and gave them a formal invitation. And when they mentioned their little babies as an excuse, they were assured that there would be a large room with beds for the babies. So the older children were all put to bed, and the three families, the Charles, Saunders, and Father and Mother assembled at our house, the three mothers in lovely evening gowns, and the babies in red flannel nighties. Each father picked up a baby and they all started for the dance.

Everything went along very nicely and they were all enjoying them-selves, when suddenly there were wild screams from the babies' room, which was a large one opening off the ballroom, with a long bed built down all one side of it, covered with mattresses and blankets, the babies being put to sleep one after the other down the length of it.

Of course every father and mother rushed toward the room when a large dog burst through the door, followed by an irate father with a baby in his arms. He aimed a kick at the dog, but unfortunately missed him, but he and the baby went sprawling. Somebody's pet dog had followed them to the dance and got into bed beside his own baby, waking up the one next to it. However, peace was soon restored and the dance went merrily on….

Shortly before we left Yale there was a very bad fire, which nearly wiped out the town, leaving only one brick store, belonging to the Oppenheimers. It was at night. All the women and children came flocking up to our house on the hill. Mama gave them tea and cocoa and made up beds for the children on the floor.

It was not long before it was built up again. The houses were very cheaply constructed in those days, just boards and cotton lined, no plaster. There were only two houses in town that were plastered; the Hudson's Bay house and the rectory.[21]

At this time Father resigned his position at Yale as he wished to get some good farming land, somewhere in the Fraser valley to locate

[to]. The government gave him his old position at Hope. He went there because it was much closer to the district in which he was trying to find suitable land. So we all went back to Hope, having been away two years, to find it a much changed place and almost deserted. The only people of our acquaintance still there were Mr. and Mrs. Pringle and Mr. and Mrs. Landvoight, and the Pringles were preparing to leave for England as they wished to have their children properly educated.[22]

Lewis Agassiz was not content living in Hope, which he viewed as a temporary situation. His heart yearned for the land; he wanted to establish a farm. In 1862, while the family travelled up the Harrison River on their way to the Cariboo, they stopped briefly along the river to pick fresh grasses for the horses. Here, Agassiz found the land of his dreams. In November that year, he filed a pre-emption on a parcel of land just east of the mouth of the Harrison River, described as "situated about 20 miles below Hope on the west side of the Fraser River opposite Indian Reserve and about one and three-quarter miles back from the river."[23] Rules for pre-empting land stated that the land must be occupied six months of the year for three years and "improvements" made. At the end of the time, with these conditions fulfilled, the land could be purchased at one dollar per acre. (This pre-emption was to be the core acquisition of the Agassiz farm; further purchases greatly increased its size.) Agassiz hired men to build a small house and clear and cultivate the land in readiness for the family's arrival. Meanwhile, the family lived in Yale and Hope. Agassiz obviously had income beyond his salary, which allowed him to invest in the land. He had a small remittance from England, possibly a family income or inheritance. This was a typical situation for many of the middle-class British immigrants during the nineteenth century whose families in England provided financial support via annual payments or remittances. Income from England was important because it offset the high cost of living in the colonies and allowed the immigrants to invest and establish homes and businesses, maintaining some semblance of middle-class authority and pretensions as gentlemen and ladies. Thus Agassiz was able to support his family, yet also establish the rudiments of a farm where they would soon live. Florence recalls this time rather differently, stating that her father searched for land after their arrival in Hope. This he most likely did, but as an addition to the holdings pre-empted in 1862.

> Leaving us in Hope, Father and a friend went exploring for land. They took a canoe and an Indian for a guide. Mr. Pringle had taken up a large tract in the name of all his children[24]—a beautiful tract covered with prairie grass with clumps of trees here and there about it like a lovely park, on which he had a family living to hold it for him. He told my father of another place near his of which he had heard. The Indians knew how to reach it and took my father down the river in a canoe then up a small hill where he had a wonderful view of the valley. My father was so enchanted with it that he lost no time filing papers on it. He then hired two men to work and put the proper amount of im-provement on it. A man was allowed to file on 160 acres to begin with and when he had proved up on that he had the option of purchasing 300 more at a dollar an acre for the whole tract....
>
> While we were still at Hope, Father engaged a man named Maxwell to take charge of the farm, paying him $60 a month, and a Chinese boy $10 to help him, and stocked the place with cows and oxen and a few horses. Maxwell was supposed to be an authority on houses, and Mother and the children were left at Hope until the house was built. This was mere supposition as we nearly perished with cold the first winter.[25]

The Agassiz family's journey from Hope to the new farm has been re-counted many times in newspaper articles and local histories for a very good reason: it was an incredibly pig-headed and risky thing to do, yet miraculously nothing went wrong. As Florence related:

> I can never forget our move from Hope. The Pringles had gone to England and we and the Landvoights were the only families left. My father wanted to ship our belongings by boat but the captain asked such an exhorbitant [sic] price that he decided to take us all down on a raft. It is hard to get anyone to believe us when we tell about it. It certainly seems like a foolhardy thing now. Father said, "Captain Irving thinks he has me in his power and can force me to pay his price."

He therefore hired two large Indian canoes, fastened them about ten feet apart and fastened planks across from one to the other, and loaded household belongings, chickens, children—everything on it. We were all very excited, as of course, were the Indians. Mother had given them all the trash that was left, to their great joy. My mother always said that Father did not know the meaning of the word "fear" and I am quite sure she did not [either], for whatever she had to go through, she never lost her sense of humor. She had given an old Indian three of her old hats. He was running about looking for a place to put them. She caught them from his hand and clapped them one on top of the other on his head, to the great amusement of the other Indians who shouted with laughter. Of course, the whole Indian village was standing about, watching proceedings. Father, who was an expert neither in a canoe or a boat, took command. He was in the stern of one boat and an Indian in the other, two squaws paddling in the bows. The other Indians helped where necessary. How we ever kept the children from falling overboard I do not know. Dick was only two years old, and determined to cast himself into the foaming waters. He strongly resented being held by his skirts or any other way. Except for his desire to jump overboard it was a most thrilling adventure. The distance was only twenty miles but rapids all the way. I am sure dear Mother must have breathed a sigh of thankfulness when we reached the first landing at the mouth of the big slough.

After reaching the Big Slough[26] landing, we had to disembark and separate the canoes as the raft was much too unwieldy to take up the slough. The bulk of the cargo was piled on the bank and the family and immediate necessities were taken to the second landing. As we landed we could see the beautiful fields of yellow grain stretched out in front of us, the men all busily reaping. Maxwell waved his cap and shouted, "Welcome to Ferny Coombe, Mrs. Agassiz!" and brought Indians and Chinamen to help us unload. Arthur, who was helping on the farm, rushed to meet us, and flung his arm around Mama in great excitement.

It was the first time Mama or the rest of us had seen the place and we were delighted with it, a beautiful valley surrounded by mountains gradually disappearing to the south. The house was built of logs, a storey and a half high. The front door opened into a good sized living room…with two bedrooms opening off it and stairs leading out of the living room, and a large kitchen lean-to at the back. Our parents and brothers occupied the downstairs bedrooms and the girls the large upstairs. It was all very rough and unfinished, with carpenter's tables, tools and sawdust still all over the floor. We all set to work sweeping and cleaning up. The stoves were put up, beds made, and children fed and put to bed. The water had to be carried from the slough as there was no well and the men were too busy with the harvest to dig one. Everyone was glad to go to bed at an early hour. We wakened in the morning with our faces frightfully swelled and eyes almost closed from mosquito bites. It was bad enough for the older ones, but the poor tiny ones suffered dreadfully. Fortunately it was September, and almost the end of the season.

It took poor Mama some time to get order out of chaos, as the men were so busy in the harvest fields they could give her no assistance. We had to carry the clothes to the slough to wash them and carry all the water for use in the house. Nelly was born in October. A horrid little French woman came from Yale to take care of poor Mama, she and her husband ran a saloon in Yale. She was furious because the baby did not arrive for three days after she did and proclaimed aloud all the good times she was missing in Yale, and went home when the baby was only five days old. We children were thankful to get her out of the house.

That was a terrible winter. The first frost cracked the clay that was stopping the chinks between the logs and the terrible blizzards from the north whistled through the house. The snow blew through and covered beds, floor and everything upstairs. All beds were brought down to the living room and sacks nailed all over the room to keep out the snow. We all yearned to mind the baby for the task meant the warmest corner by the stove. The snow drifted into the kitchen. We had to keep our heads and shoulders wrapped to protect them. The water that splashed from the dishpan froze on the table. The bread sponge set by the stove to rise, would freeze on the one side and scorch on the other. Fortunately the well had been dug before the cold weather started. It was very primitive, a square box put around the top, a round hole in the box through which a stout rope was drawn and knotted, the other end fastened to a metal bucket and the water was drawn up hand over hand. We kept two buckets on a bench in the kitchen full of water. When I was in charge of the kitchen I always kept one eye on these buckets and the other out of the window and when the water began to get low I would hail an Indian or Chinaman and present him the buckets to be refilled.... An Indian woman with her baby on her back would walk across the river on the ice every Monday morning to do the washing. They did not seem to mind it at all. They got two meals and fifty cents and often a piece of liver or kidney (from the slaughtered pigs). Sometimes her husband would come and shoot a couple of grouse which was a great treat after unlimited salt pork and salmon. My mother taught all of the women to knit and bake bread. The only money they ever saw was what they got from us for washing, shooting, catching salmon, and working in the fields. I don't know what we would have done without them. The Indian village of Cheam was on the other side of the river and that is where Bill Bristol,[27] the express and mail carrier, always left our mail. After several years there was a telegraph office there also.

That first winter, as I have already mentioned, was terribly cold, and it was very late before the ice broke up. We were entirely out of flour and coal oil. We had to grind wheat in a tiny pepper mill screwed to the wall and we made candles from beeswax and tallow. We had candle molds which we threaded with cotton wick and tied at the ends to keep the hot tallow from running out at the blunt end. We put the looped wick over sticks and when they were cold and hard we cut the knots off and pulled the candles out. When burning the wicks would grow long and unsightly and had to be constantly snuffed, for which we had a pretty pair of silver snuffers standing in a silver tray which my sisters still have.

The wolves used to circle around the house at night and their blood-curdling howls would frighten the little ones and often wake them up at night screaming. They often struck terror into my heart also; I really never heard those terrible howls without cringing....

We never experienced a blizzard before that winter. The cold blast came down through a gap in the mountain. It was next to impossible to stand against it. It piled the snow in tremendous drifts. It would have been very exciting if it were not that my brothers had to struggle against it in their outdoor tasks, feeding the stock and milking the cows. We all felt happy when the first spring rains came, melting the snow and then it was not long until the beautiful wild flowers sprang up on mountainside and in the valley. My mother laid out a nice vegetable garden after the land had been grubbed and plowed. The soil was very rich and it was not long before we had all sorts of green vegetables. Spring brought lots of work, the men plowing and sowing, and Mother with the help of Jinny and me did the housework, cooked, made butter, looked after the garden and tended the chickens. There was no more play except for the little ones. My father had a high picket fence built around the house to keep the children safe.

We were up at five every morning. My brothers milked the cows while we got breakfast; they taking theirs with the men in the kitchen; Father, Mother and we girls having ours in the dining room. So the days went on until the hot weather melted the snow from the mountains, swelling the Fraser to overflowing and filling all the sloughs that ran here and there through the valley, making it quite difficult to get about. About the first of July it began to subside and then came the plague of mosquitoes. It is impossible for anyone who has not had experience with them to imagine the torture they were. We did not have the wire screening they have now. We had to tack mosquito netting over the windows and burn smudges in the rooms and even then our faces, hands and legs were swelled out of shape. The poor children would scratch them until they were raw....

The nights were worse than the days with mosquitoes. They had been known to kill calves. Sometimes they were so thick that it was difficult to breathe without getting them in your mouth or nose. This would last until the middle of September. Since this time the building of dykes and clearing of the land has almost done away with the pests.[28]

As the eldest girl in a family that ultimately included 10 children, Florence was needed greatly by her mother to assist with child rearing and domestic duties. Her *Memories* provide many details of long work days, chores and especially her responsibilities as a seamstress. Each child required clothing, either adapted through skillful tailoring from a sibling's hand-me-down, or cut out and sewn by hand from material purchased in Yale or New Westminster.

Angela College, the Anglican girls' school in Victoria, 1865.
PHOTOGRAPHER: EDWARD DOSSETER. B.C. ARCHIVES C-3857.

In 1868, at the age of fourteen, Florence, accompanied by her father, left Ferny Coombe, travelling by steamer along the Fraser to New Westminster and then boarding another steamer bound for Victoria. She was going to school, living in residence at the Anglican-church-sponsored Angela College. It was her first formal education apart from infrequent attendance at Mrs. Glennie's school in Hope.[29] Her mother had acted as tutor, teaching all the children the rudiments of reading and writing. Florence must have been a good scholar, as the arrangement with Angela College was that she would teach the youngest class in exchange for the tuition costs of her own instruction. She would not leave home without one final adventure.

The fall term opened in September. Mother went to Yale to get me some clothes. She was taken to the landing in the oxsled to wait for the steamer. The steamer always came on Monday and Friday but erratic as to the hour, as they had to make many landings taking on and putting off freight. There were no docks or wharfs. The boat just ran up to the bank and men ran a plank out for the passengers to walk on. Mother was very much pleased when she went on board to find Mr. O'Reilly and several friends which made her trip very pleasant. They were the first white faces she had seen since leaving Hope. When she reached home she said, "I did have such a delightful time. I don't think I stopped talking from the time I stepped on board until I reached Yale."

I was having a birthday (my fourteenth) before I left, so we four elder children climbed a small mountain near the house to celebrate with a picnic. We told our parents we would light a fire to show them how far up we had got. Arthur gathered a few sticks and put a match to it and it seemed to me that in about half a minute the whole mountainside was in flames. We had a hard time getting down alive, Arthur took the hands of the two youngest and I followed, racing over rocks and boulders until we finally reached safety at the bottom. My father and mother were relieved to see us. There was a fire raging on the other side of the river. We never dreamed that our little blaze would set our own side on fire…. My father was out most of the night fighting it with the Indians and Chinamen. He had a barn full of hay and grain on the bank of the river, already sold, and waiting to be shipped to Yale. They had to plow all around it for some distance and back [up the] fire. They fortunately saved the barn.

Just before I left for Victoria there was a heavy rain which put out most of the fires but for several days the smoke and fog was so dense that we would get lost crossing the field. When the day arrived for me to leave I was frantically excited. Father accompanied me to Victoria. We walked from the dock to Angela College, the name of the school. It had a high board fence all around it. Miss Pemberton,[30] the principal, was a frail and delicate little woman, very kind and gentle, and I liked her very much. I had a happy time the few months I was there. There were girls from all parts of the country…. I had at that time very long and luxuriant hair, only six inches from the floor. Long hair was thought a lot of in those days. When I arrived, Miss Pemberton took me to my room to tidy up for dinner. She told me just to brush my hair out and leave it hanging down. All of my sisters had a lot of hair and having known very few other girls, I was quite unprepared for the surprised exclamations that greeted me, and every girl made an excuse to pass my chair and lift my hair as it lay several inches on the floor around me. This will seem strange to young people of this day and age, who far prefer short hair. I must say mine was a good deal of a nuisance at times. It was always tumbling down at the most inconvenient times, playing prisoner's base and running games like that. We used to ride a great deal on the farm and it did not matter how tightly I tied and pinned it, as soon as we stretched into a good gallop, down it came over the back of the horse.

The boarders at the school were all a very sweet lot of girls and were kindness personified. They were all a long way from their own homes and I have no doubt had suffered a lot from homesickness. I was very happy and contented. On Friday evenings we used to dance or get up little plays and I was always very much pleased because I was asked to take part in them. I was in the highest class in all English studies and second in French. There were two other girls in the class of my age, the others were all much older, up to seventeen. They would all crowd into my room after we were supposed to be in bed while I told them stories from the Waverly novels, Dickens, Arabian Nights, etc. I don't think any of them had read very much for they always seemed so thrilled with the stories I told them….

During the Christmas holidays some friends of my parents asked me to stay with them and I was asked to all of the Christmas festivities. The greatest event for the young people was a large Twelfth Night Ball at Government House. Oh, the wonderful joy of it! There were two men-of-war at Esquimalt and crowds of middies. My friends lived just over the hedge from Government House, their name was Stallschmidts,[31] English people with two daughters of my age. We all went to the ball. I am afraid the poor young boys of the town did not have a very good time as the naughty girls had eyes for nothing but brass buttons that night. I was almost delirious with joy. It seemed as if it must be a dream. I went to so many parties through the holidays. It was a delight to write home and tell all about it. The postage was twenty-five cents a letter. I wrote once a week.[32]

In March 1869 Florence was told she must return to Ferny Coombe. Her mother was expecting her ninth child and the family responsibilities weighed heavily. Disappointed at the shortness of her education and very sad to leave all her new friends, Florence returned home. It was to be several years more until she would return to Victoria and resume her friendships, but meanwhile she maintained an active correspondence, persevering over time to develop the friendships begun at school.

Mother and my brothers and sisters were all happy to have me with them again and I had so much to tell them about all the friends I had made and the wonders of the city, the men-of-war and all of my gay experiences. Of course I went home to grueling hard work which was shared by all, even the tiny ones who could pick up chips to start the fire or hold a dishtowel. I taught the little ones now, most of my school friends wrote to me, and Mother encouraged me to write to them. Their letters were always a great pleasure to both my sister Jinny and me....

That September in the middle of harvest, and on my fifteenth birthday, my sister Lue was born. Mother was not able to get a nurse. An Indian woman had to take the baby and poor Mama attended to it herself, and I had to bathe and dress the poor little one and care for my mother who was very ill. There were twenty men in the harvest field to be cooked for, bread baked, twenty pounds of butter to be churned every other day, a large flock of chickens to be looked after besides the housework and the children to be taken care of. Jinny was only thirteen but took entire charge of the chickens, children and room work. I took care of Mama and baby, cooking, baking and dairy. My brothers did the milking. James was only eleven. Jinny (Jane) helped with the milk pans and buckets, Minnie and Connie, six and seven, dried dishes. It was a long time before dear Mother was strong again. It must have been terrible for her, she had always tried to spare us as much as possible, but she had come to a place where the best help she could give was to keep perfectly quiet and as cheerful as possible.

But it was a good lesson for me. Dear Jinny was always unselfish and bright and gay, but I was impatient and inclined to be rebellious at our hard lot. I found out then that it was the dear mother who was bearing the heaviest burden and was always sweet and uncomplaining and that she was the one who had to be watched over and loved, she who had always been sheltered, loved and admired, to be living such a desperately lonely, poverty-stricken life, never the sight of a white face

Florence and her sister Jinny (Jane), ca. 1874.
PHOTOGRAPHER: UNKNOWN. PRIVATE COLLECTION.

beyond her family from one year's end to the other, and her one thought was to get the best out of it all for her children.

Every day she and Father held family prayers morning and evening, and on Sunday morning the regular church service, Mother reading a sermon written by some brilliant divine. I have often heard some wayfarer, stopping over night, say he had heard "Mrs. Agassiz preach a better sermon than he had ever heard at church." She tried to instill us with character and principles, also she would take time to drill us to stand and walk correctly. Many are the hours I have spent manipulating a back board with a book on my head, or coming quietly in the door closing it gently behind me, with a smile on my face to greet the imagined company. She trained us even to make a court curtsey which was considered part of every lady's education. Of course we were rather inclined to make a joke of the latter performance. Mother would laugh with us but insisted that it be done properly and it certainly stood us in good stead. I was presented to the Governor General and his wife, Lord and Lady Dufferin, when they visited in Victoria many years later....[33]

In the autumn of 1875 Florence's brother Arthur, who had assumed much of the management of the farms, had a dreadful accident. In the midst of threshing, his sleeve was caught in the cog wheels and his arm drawn through the machine and completely severed. He was rushed down river to New Westminster and the surgeon. Mrs. Agassiz stayed with Arthur a month while he recuperated, and she then returned to the farm. Arthur remained another month in New Westminster and boarded with the Woods family until he was strong enough to travel.[34] Florence was there also, assisting Mrs. Woods care for her children who had all come down with childhood illnesses at one time.

> Mrs. Woods was a very delicate woman. She had thirteen children and she also taught a number of young girls at a day school. It was quite late in November. It was nearly two months since Arthur's accident, the weather turned bitterly cold, with a raging snowstorm. We had to make arrangements to return at once as the river usually froze and stopped navigation when it turned so cold....
>
> The next day we left for home. It was a dreadful day, frightfully cold, the wind blowing a hurricane and the river full of floating ice. The captain could not take the boat past the mouth of the Harrison River, he was afraid of being crushed in the ice. Bill Bristol, who was on board in charge of the mail and express, hired a large canoe and two Indians. Arthur and I were wrapped in blankets and put in the

canoe, [and] the captain blew a number of blasts of the whistle hoping it would be heard at Agassiz, ten miles away, and bring someone out to meet us. It took several hours to go those ten miles, I forget really how long it was. We had a large hot meal before we left the boat. I don't remember feeling in the least frightened although it took all one Indian could do to fend the enormous cakes of ice off the canoe, while Bristol and the other Indian paddled with all their strength against the rapid current. At last late at night we made the landing and found James there to meet us. He had a large fire on the point to guide us and an ox-sled to tuck us into. In another half hour or three-quarters we were at home, the house warm and bright, and a delicious warm meal waiting for us. How happy dear Mother was to see us safe at home again, Arthur none the worse for his trying journey.[35]

In 1876 Florence was invited by Mrs. Charles, her former neighbour in Hope, to visit and stay with them in Victoria for the summer. Florence's younger sister Jinny (Jane) had been invited the previous year. Mabel Charles, although younger than Florence, became a good friend and together they attended many social functions, including those coordinated for the visit of the Governor General of Canada, the Earl of Dufferin. Parties at Government House, naval entertainments, picnics, parades and tennis—it was a whirlwind summer, and at the end of it, Florence was engaged.

I can never forget the joy of that summer. Staying with Mrs. Charles, I was of course, included in all of the festivities except dinners. The Dufferins came by rail to San Francisco, where they boarded a British Man-of-war for Esquimalt. There they were met by the Governor and Mrs. Trutch, Premier Elliot and all of the leading people. They drove to the outskirts of Victoria where the parade started and marched through town to Government House. The navy and middies with their bands, the police and firemen, school children carrying long silken banners, and the Chinese with musical instruments. Everyone cheered wildly.

The next day, or rather evening, the earl and countess held a drawing room. For months before all of the ladies had been in a state of excitement about their dresses and court trains. Mrs. Charles who was a beautiful woman with shoulders like white velvet, wore a beautiful black velvet with white lace. Mine was an old pale pink silk which one of my aunts had worn to Queen Victoria's court, made over with lots of pink illusion. It really looked lovely—at least all my friends said it did, but there was such a crowd and so many beautiful dresses it was no doubt quite unnoticed. Two days after, Lady Dufferin held a small reception at Government House—only the elite of the town were at it. It was a delightful affair. Lady Dufferin was graciousness personified. She chatted pleasantly with each and everyone and left a delightful impression upon all who met her, as also did the earl. He, of course, was a trained diplomat, being a wise and clever statesman. He realized the great need of a railway to unite the east with the minerally wealthy west.[36]

That summer, Florence met John Goodfellow (1841–1912), manager of the Bank of British North America. Thirteen years her senior, Goodfellow was a very eligible bachelor. To Florence perhaps, he represented the excitement of society and a life she did not have at home.

He returned with her to Ferny Coombe to meet her family and press for an early marriage. A compromise between the next spring, which Florence's mother wished, and immediately, which Goodfellow advocated, was determined. On 27 November, after an autumn filled with sewing and preparations, the two were married at Ferny Coombe by Archdeacon Woods.[37] The service was scheduled for Sunday at seven in the morning so they could catch the nine o'clock boat for New Westminster and on to Victoria. In Victoria another reception was held, and then the newlyweds settled into the big Bank of British North America house, which contained "ten large rooms and a ballroom. There were four acres of land, which included a large orchard with the best of everything in the way of fruit, a large kitchen garden, lawn, shrubbery and flowers."[38]

As wife of a prominent citizen, Florence was immediately thrust into the social whirl of Victoria. She enjoyed it all immensely and in the next year bore a son, and the following year, a daughter. In 1880 John Goodfellow was transferred to Portland, Oregon, and the family left British Columbia. Florence bore 11 children over the years and never did return to Canada. She died in Seattle in 1940 at the age of 86.

John Goodfellow, ca. 1879.
PHOTOGRAPHER: BRADLEY & RULOFSON,
SAN FRANCISCO. B.C. ARCHIVES G-8477.

Florence Goodfellow (née Agassiz), ca.
1877. PHOTOGRAPHER: S.A. SPENCER,
VICTORIA. B.C. ARCHIVES G-8479.

Florence Agassiz's recollections give a view of colonial childhood that was in part controlled by the actions of parents. The opportunities for personal expansion were much more limited because of this structured setting. For women and children in isolated settlements, the daily routine of life and farm operations used up most of the time and energies. Florence's mother appears in the writings as a strong personality. It is she who drew the line at a foolish attempt to transport a young family, ill-equipped, on an unknown Cariboo Road. It is she who bore 10 children over a 19-year period and bravely endured many births far from medical assistance. It is she who schooled all 10 children, learned to bake and cook under unfavourable conditions and yet sheltered her eldest daughters from the real burden of domestic duties to allow them some childhood freedoms. The extent of her mother's responsibilities came as quite a shock to Florence during her mother's illness in 1869.

In contrast, Florence mentions her father only within the context of certain anecdotes, which are not complimentary. For example: "My father made a dismal failure of the farm (on Prince Edward Island)" and "he tried several businesses but did not do well at any of them."[39] She never once discusses him as an individual as she did her mother. He seems to have been inclined to avoid responsibilities, relying on others to run the farm for him.

Certainly, Florence's brother Arthur was thrust into responsibilities at an early age. "My brothers worked desperately hard, they were so young and worked from 5 am. to 6 pm. and often much later when there was a press of work."[40] While still a teenager, Arthur had to be sent to Victoria for several weeks rest because he was so "run down and overworked and needed a change and rest...he was only seventeen at this time and James eleven. Arthur could do a man's work and James could drive the oxen."[41] Florence's dismissal of her father is better understood with the knowledge of these years. In 1875, Lewis Agassiz left behind his wife, his children—who ranged in age from two and a half years to twenty-two years old—and his farm and travelled to visit his mother in England. The visit complete, he embarked, not on a direct route back to Canada, but on a five-year world tour, ostensibly a roundabout way home via Europe and Asia. He visited his brother, an officer with the English fleet at Constantinople, and in July 1880 "died from the effects of sunstroke while hunting in Asia Minor."[42] He was buried in Acre, Syria.[43] It was several months before the news made its way back to British Columbia, and by then, the family was presumably either quite frantic with worry over his absence or resigned to the situation. An absent father, the reality of a hard existence on the farm and the isolation of the family undoubtedly played a part in Florence's decision to marry as quickly as she did.

Florence's writing is split into two sections. The majority of the text is written in the third person as she distanced herself from the story to present a clear overview of the family's early history in Hope and Yale. She was writing her family history at the request of her children, so she did not insert personal opinion into this section. In fact, it is almost devoid of personal feelings. The episodes she recalls are obviously the highlights or the most vivid of her childhood memories. It is not until the

Some members of the Agassiz family at Ferny Coombe, ca. 1890. This group does not include Florence, who was then living in the United States. STANDING L TO R: Eleanor Maud (Nell); Lewis Arthur (who lost his arm in a threshing accident); Mary Louisa (Minnie); Wing, the Chinese house-boy; John R. Brown, husband of Luella. SEATED L TO R: Luella Beatrice Agassiz Brown with infant son; Mary Caroline Agassiz (née Schram), mother of the family; Constance Teresa (Connie). PHOTOGRAPHER: UNKNOWN. PRIVATE COLLECTION.

last portion of her *Memories* that she begins to tell about herself and switches to the first person. This is the time when she draws in on herself as the focus, and here we learn of her feelings—the disappointments and the trials, the joys and the exhilaration. Her accounts of life in Victoria for schooling, her time in New Westminster and trip home with Arthur, and her subsequent visits to Victoria are all strong episodes in her growing years. They explain and define the reality of her life in isolated Ferny Coombe and contrast it with the excitement and opportunities of the social scene in Victoria. This prepares the reader for the eventual meeting

Florence Agassiz Goodfellow in her eighties, ca.1935.
PHOTOGRAPHER: MCBRIDE & ANDERSON, SEATTLE. PRIVATE COLLECTION.

with her future husband. At this point she sums up in a single page the transformation from eldest daughter to young wife. And here, her *Memories* rather abruptly conclude, as if from this point on, her family already knew the story.

NOTES

1 Florence Goodfellow, *Memories of Pioneer Life in British Columbia*, typescript, B.C. Archives, 1929–1933, published privately 1941 and later published by the Kent Centennial Committee, 1958. Quotes cited are from the 1958 publication.

2 Agassiz was first a commissioned officer in the Royal Welsh Fusiliers, which he abandoned in favour of farming a fully stocked Prince Edward Island farm, purchased previously by his father for the two eldest sons. Failing dismally at this, he and his wife returned to her home in London, Canada West, "where he tried several businesses but did not do well at any of them." Ibid., p. 7.

3 James Douglas (1803–1877), Chief Factor of the Hudson's Bay Company, Governor of the Colony of Vancouver Island, and later of the mainland Colony of British Columbia. Douglas and his family were at the centre of social life in Victoria. He retired in 1864 and was knighted for his many years of service.

4 "The Agassiz of Agassiz," *The Province*, 11 September 1948.

5 The introduction of camels to British Columbia in 1862 represents one of the oddest episodes and the most unusual entrepreneurial effort. Camels were imported because it was thought that they would make good pack animals along the trail to the gold fields. What was unaccounted for, however, was that their feet were not suited to the rocky terrain, and their smell frightened the horses and other pack animals they encountered, which created mass confusion and chaos. It was soon apparent that the scheme was a failure.

6 Charles Stubbert Finlaison (1827–1906) came to Victoria in 1859. Many years later he married Jane Holmes (1860–1926), and they raised a family of nine children.

7 Captain Jamieson was one of four brothers involved in steamboats.

8 *Memories*, pp. 7–13.

9 "The Agassiz of Agassiz."

10 Edward Howard Sanders (1832–1902) arrived in Victoria in the spring of 1859 and was appointed Justice of the Peace, then in May, stipendiary judge at Yale. In 1864 he became a member of the first Legislative Council of British Columbia. That same year he married Annie Moresby, former governess to the Pringle children in Hope. Noted in Margaret Ormsby, *A Pioneer Gentlewoman in British Columbia* (Vancouver: University of British Columbia Press, 1991), p. 97.

11 Rev. A.D. Pringle (1828–1908) arrived in Hope in August 1859. His wife, Marie Louisa, and two daughters arrived in Victoria from England in August the following year. In 1864, after the birth of two more daughters and a son and a falling out with the Bishop, the Pringles left the colony and returned to England. *A Pioneer Gentlewoman*, p. 96.

12 Christ Church at Hope was endowed by Baroness Angela Burdett-Coutts. Designed by Captain J.M. Grant of the Royal Engineers, it was built in 1861.

13 William Charles (1831–1903) was in charge of the Hudson's Bay Company (H.B.C.) at Fort Hope in 1860, then, successively, Forts Yale and Kamloops. In 1874 he was promoted to oversee all H.B.C. operations in the Western Depot and was resident in Victoria. He married Mary Ann (née Birnie), and they had one daughter, Mabel (after whom Mabel Lake is apparently named), born in 1860. The Charleses were great friends with the Agassiz family. *A Pioneer Gentlewoman*, pp. 90–91.

14 George and Mary Landvoight arrived in British Columbia in 1858, establishing a store at Hope. Later Landvoight became postmaster and Justice of the Peace. In February 1878, he was killed in an accident at the sawmill in Hope. *A Pioneer Gentlewoman*, p. 93.

15 Thomas Glennie, accompanied by his wife and her daughters Jane and Susan, arrived in Hope in 1860. He promptly pre-empted land on the Coquihalla River and began improvements and construction of a log house called Hopelands. Glennie soon became hopelessly in debt and made plans to leave the colony, but not before he cleverly managed to obtain title to the 160 acres of land, which were sold at auction to pay his debts. Mrs. Glennie and her daughters were penniless. They moved to New Westminster, but in 1867, Susan and her mother returned to Hope, lived in the former Pringle home and opened a school. It is possible that Florence Agassiz may have attended this school for a very short time. See *A Pioneer Gentlewoman* for further elaboration of the Glennie saga.

16 Hope was the terminus of the H.B.C. Brigade Trail, over which furs were transported from the hinterland to the coast, and the Dewdney Trail, which led through the Okanagan to the Kootenay mining area.

17 Harriet Oppenheimer was a daughter of Charles Oppenheimer (1832–1890). Oppenheimer and his brothers operated several supply houses. In 1858 he moved to Yale and constructed a warehouse and store (the foundations of which can be seen today). In 1862 he became a contractor for the Cariboo Wagon Road and, in 1873, retired from business and moved to San Francisco. *A Pioneer Gentlewoman*, p. 97.

18 Joseph and John Trutch were partners on various road-building contracts, constructing sections of the Cariboo Wagon Road. John eventually worked for Andrew Onderdonk on the Canadian Pacific Railway construction; Joseph went on to become Lieutenant Governor of British Columbia.

19 The Alexandra Suspension bridge over the Fraser River at Spuzzum was a marvel of engineering construction. It was designed by Joseph Trutch and opened in 1862, remaining until 1894, when the spring freshet wiped it out.

20 The Frenchman five miles out of Yale may be the "old Frenchman" described by Sarah Crease in 1880. See Kathryn Bridge, *Henry & Self: An English Gentlewoman at the Edge of Empire*, (Victoria: Sono Nis Press, 1996; Royal BC Museum, 2019), pp. 189, 192.

21 The rectory was adjacent to St. John the Divine, built in 1860 by the Royal Engineers.

22 *Memories*, pp. 12–20.

23 Quoted in J.J. Woods, *The Agassiz Harrison Valley, History and Development* (Kent: Kent Historical Committee, 1958), p.3.

24 Apparently Pringle pre-empted three parcels of land for his daughters, but left the colony before completing the requirements for improvements. *A Pioneer Gentlewoman*, p. 96.

25 *Memories*, pp. 20-21.

26 This was later known as the Agassiz Slough.

27 "Captain" William Yale Bristol, express and mail carrier for many years, originally had a farm on Bristol Island, west of Hope. The express service was more lucrative, handling mail, goods and passengers on a canoe service along the waterways between Yale and New Westminster. *A Pioneer Gentlewoman*, p. 109.

28 *Memories*, pp. 21–26.

29 See note 15.

30 Miss Pemberton, headmistress of the Church of England–sponsored Angela College, resigned her position in the spring of 1869 and left the colony. In the advanced stages of consumption, she died in France the following year. See chapter on Helen Kate Woods.

31 Thomas Lett Stahlschmidt (d. 1888), a successful commission merchant, and his family lived in Victoria and were active in the social scene. Stahlschmidt acted as British Columbia Agent-General in London for several years. The two girls Agassiz refers to are Florence and Mary Pauline, daughters of Edward Hammond King (d. 1861) and Mrs. Stahlschmidt (King's widow).

32 *Memories*, pp. 26–28.

33 Ibid., pp. 29–31.

34 Woods family. See notes in chapter on Helen Kate Woods.

35 *Memories*, p. 39.

36 Ibid., pp. 40–41.

37 *Mainland Guardian*, 29 November 1876.

38 *Memories*, pp. 42–43.

39 Ibid., p. 7.

40 Ibid., p. 31.

41 Ibid.

42 Information from an undated memo written by Lewis Arthur Agassiz. Vertical Files, B.C. Archives.

43 *British Colonist*, 26 September 1880, p. 3.

ELEANOR CAROLINE

fellows

1831–1926

Portrait of Eleanor Fellows, ca. 1862–1866. PRIVATE COLLECTION.

ELEANOR CAROLINE FELLOWS was born on 1 March 1831 at Bruce Castle, Tottenham, Middlesex, England, to Caroline Pearson and Rowland Hill. She was the second of four children and grew up amid an extended family of aunts, uncles and cousins. Her father and his brothers, pioneer educators, established a series of model schools that were renowned for the innovative practice of self-government by students and the abolition of corporal punishment.[1] Consequently, her family life was intertwined with rich educational opportunities, important in shaping Eleanor's personality and making her an outspoken, well-read, opinionated and passionate woman. Eleanor's father, Rowland Hill, moved on from schooling, achieving recognition in the Colonial Office and later as a postal reformer. His invention of penny postage revolutionized nineteenth-century communication by mail, earning him a knighthood conferred by Queen Victoria in 1860.

In 1846–47 Eleanor and several schoolmates spent a year in France under the guardianship of an Englishwoman. While there, Eleanor perfected her language skills and was exposed to opera, an art form that would have a lasting influence and importance in her life. Returning to England, she attended art classes, learning sketching, watercolours and sculpting,[2] but her passion was the Italian opera, and she took lessons from Mme. Lablache, whose father-in-law was Queen Victoria's singing master and friend. Mme. Lablache appears to have excelled as a singing master and as a teacher. Eleanor found her system "so admirable and her taste so pure that her pupils learned to condemn any but first-rate vocalists."[3]

In October 1861 Eleanor married Arthur Fellows,[4] a son of Isaac Fellows, headmaster at one of the Hill family schools. Nothing is known of their courtship, but in addition to the teaching connection, the two families were previously united through the marriage of Eleanor's older sister Louisa to Arthur's brother Frank, in 1856.

The marriage of Eleanor and Arthur took place only months after Fellows had returned to England from time spent in San Francisco and Victoria, where he and his brother Alfred owned hardware businesses. The brothers had spent the previous two years establishing first a partnership, and then separate firms, which advertised their affiliations with "the House of F.P. Fellows & Co."[5]

Brother Frank's Wolverhampton business supplied their far-off colonial business directly, an advertising and marketing move that made it possible to sell merchandise in Victoria at a lower price than their competitors by cutting out the San Francisco middlemen. A hardware business was certainly needed in Victoria at this time. In 1858 the settlement had grown almost overnight from a white population of some 500 individuals to 25,000 with the influx of miners en route to the gold diggings on the Fraser River.[6]

Arthur and Alfred remained in Victoria from 1859 until the spring of 1861, when they both returned to England. Perhaps Arthur and Eleanor wrote to each other during these years and perhaps had made commitments to each other. Unfortunately, no evidence exists to prove or disprove this supposition, although the fact that Eleanor married Arthur Fellows only months after his return from Victoria indicates a certain familiarity! Shortly after the wedding, Eleanor, Arthur, Alfred and his wife, Louisa (née Morgan), left England on the steamer *Niagara* bound for British Columbia.[7] Eleanor recounted:

> Only towards the end of 1861 did I see my day-dreams realised; and that was when I married, and set out for British Columbia, and in those days a long six-weeks' journey, involving many steamer-changes and the crossing by rail of the Isthmus of Panama. Then at last did I come to taste the ocean salt upon my lips, and feel the ocean-breezes ruffle my hair and bring colour to my face; then did I sway from head to foot in unison with the lively dance of the good steam-ship *Niagara* as she breasted the eastward-flowing, huge waves of the Atlantic in November.
>
> "Rough!" exclaimed a pleasantly-smiling, toughened old salt, in answer to a remark I, one day, hazarded, while, for a brief space, I lay

prostrate in a deck-chair; for we had set out in a "half-gale" which bore a surprisingly strong family likeness to a whole one, "Why, it's only really rough when you get three waves to a quarter of a mile!"....

Our ship took fourteen days to bridge the tumbling seas between Liverpool and Boston. But ocean "grey-hounds" capable of performing the trip in less than half that time were as yet unknown. Therefore the opinion on board was unanimous that, with persistent head-winds and heavy weather all the way, we had not fared amiss....

From Boston we went to New York, and thence by steamer to Colon on the Isthmus of Panama.... The making of the great fifty-odd miles long canal which now connects two oceans is without doubt a triumph of engineering skill, a world-wonder which would have amazed even those masters of scientific construction and of the universe so far as it was known to them, the Romans. But the work has involved, perhaps necessitated, the perpetration of one act of vandalism much to be deplored, the obliteration, maybe permanent, of most of the beautiful Isthmian scenery.... When, on a sultry December day I first beheld the Isthmus, it seemed like fairy land, only that one very unfairylike feature had strayed into the picture. For on the Changres river's unlovely, bare-looking, muddy banks reposed scores of alligators resembling large, roughly-hewn logs of wood, and about as motionless, feigning slumber, but always, 'tis said, with eyes half open, watching for a favourable opportunity to get a sudden snap at any unwary pedestrian, biped or quadruped, who should come within reach. But the jungle, then abundant, was beautiful, with thickets of graceful, bower-like trees and flower-laden undergrowth, all laced together by blossoming parasitic festoons; with here and there a tiny village, a stream, or placid lake; and the steadfast, violet-tinted mountain-range making a scarcely varying background to the ever-changing scene lying at its feet. For several hours we sat on the leisurely-moving train traversing the forty miles of winding railway, watched the fascinating landscape, and consumed the luscious fruit which, whenever a stoppage was made to feed our insatiable locomotive with its wooden diet the picturesquely-clad natives importuned us to buy. An unforgettable scene after snow-and-ice-bound Boston and New York quitted so recently....

In due course (we were shipped) on board the very worst of the several bad Vanderbilt steamers on which I have made a voyage.... We had lately crossed the Atlantic in a Cunarder; and although the steamers of that line were then far from being the palatial floating hotels they have since become, the contrast between the one on which we had spent fourteen days in comfort—and that one as second-rate liner only—and any of the Vanderbilters I have known was amazing. Some of these latter ought not to have gone to sea at all.... The accommodation in saloon and cabins was very poor, while as regards certain other necessary accommodation it was...entirely wanting. The bedding was mean and scanty; and the food provided...even for the first-class passengers was insufficient, uninviting, and not too cleanly served. When it became apparent that the ship's officers, one of whom sat at each end of the several first-class tables, had rather better fare than we, including milk for the strange beverages inappropriately called tea and coffee, a spirit of revolt broke out among us, and whenever the chance occurred we raided the table-end supplies until defeated by superior force or more skilful strategy. How the second-class people fared for food I do not know, but was told that for the steerage it was a case of "toujours perdrix," only that, instead of those toothsome birds, very weak gruel was doled out three times a day in very slender portions; a fact which indeed I witnessed more than once.... The cabins which the passengers of the intermediate class should have occupied, and for which they had paid, were filled with freight even before their rightful tenants went on board at Panama. The victims had perforce to sleep wherever they could lie or sit, in nooks and corners upon deck, or on the heaped-up luggage which should have been consigned to the hold. When in the evening we walked the deck in the bright moonlight then prevailing, it was not always easy to avoid treading on the sleepers. To undress, or to change any but outer clothing must have been to many all but impossible.... I have, of set purpose, reproduced this unpleasing picture because it serves to illustrate some of the evils of monopoly; and because it is indicative of the heartlessness and greed of which those can be guilty who wield almost unlimited power under its aegis....

For close upon a fortnight we endured these discomforts as best we could, though with ever-deepening indignation; and then one day, to our intense relief, the Golden Gate was sighted, and we bent to eastward....[8]

From San Francisco, Eleanor and her husband boarded the *Cortez*, bound for Esquimalt Harbour on Vancouver Island where they arrived on 6 January 1862.[9] Following such eventful voyages, it must have been pure relief to finally arrive.

> During my stay throughout most of the 'sixties in British Columbia (or rather Vancouver Island), then in its youth as a separated and sparsely-peopled Colony cut off from eastern and central Canada almost as effectively as if it had been in another planet, I came in some ways to get a backward peep into the Britain of our early English, or as some people, with doubtful accuracy, prefer to call them, "Saxon," days.
>
> Little Victoria, the capital, must have been not unlike our own infant settlements in Britain of a thousand and many more years past, in that it was a wooden town of unpretentious buildings which, except where it faced the sea, was hemmed in by vast forests whose outer fringe only had been explored, and in which roamed packs of fierce timber wolves and other beasts of prey....[10]

View of Victoria, Vancouver Island, 1860. The town of Victoria grew up and quickly surrounded the old fort. The palisade walls of the fort were finally demolished in 1862.
ARTIST: H.O. TIEDEMANN. B.C. ARCHIVES PDP01538.

The Fellows first took up residence on Birdcage Walk (today's Government Street) in a small house facing the quaintly constructed wooden Legislative Buildings, nicknamed "the Birdcages" because of their unusual architectural mix. The house stood on land adjacent to the home of James Douglas, then Governor of the colonies of Vancouver Island and British Columbia. Arthur resumed management of the hardware business and also advertised as a commission merchant.[11] From newspaper accounts, it is evident that Arthur, like many other merchants at the time, travelled between Victoria and San Francisco on a regular basis, leaving Eleanor behind in Victoria.[12] During her first Victoria year, Eleanor must have had much free time.

Eleanor gave birth to her first children, twin daughters, approximately 18 months after her arrival in the colony. Up to this point she was unfettered by family responsibilities and therefore had the leisure to write, explore and develop relationships with her social set and also delve into the mysteries of those of other cultures. Her husband's business prospered through the Cariboo gold rush of 1862, which, like the earlier rush of 1858, brought thousands of miners through Victoria, where they had to obtain mining licences before heading to the diggings.

Eleanor's twin daughters Mary Clara and Caroline Frances were born on 30 July 1863.[13] Soon the house on Birdcage Walk became too small for a growing family. In July 1864, an advertisement in the *British Colonist* attracted their attention. "Thetis Cottage, near Craigflower and on Esquimalt Harbour in good condition, partly furnished and suitable for a family, on most reasonable terms."[14] The Fellows family arranged to lease Thetis Cottage and moved in later that year. On 2 April 1865 a son, Rowland Hill, was born, followed a year later by another son, Arthur.[15]

In 1916, at the age of 85, Eleanor privately published *An Octogenarian's Reminiscences*, which she had completed in manuscript form two years earlier. Eleanor recounted various incidents and adventures in her life, utilizing the many letters and notes written years before. She included several chapters about her life in Victoria and the people she knew.[16] Eleanor recounts the motivation for publishing her memoirs:

> At different times during the past years, some of my friends—one a successful authoress—unto whom, as is my wont, I had been spinning my old yarns, have said "Why don't you write your Reminiscences?" Invariably I have answered the question a l'Ecossaise, by asking another—"Would anyone read them?"
>
> But later it struck me that as in the course of a long life fate had brought me into contact with some rather uncommon experiences and with people as uncommon, it might be worth while to draw upon

that mental storehouse, Memory, and make of the material extracted a volume which perchance others besides my friends would care to read.[17]

This was not Eleanor's first foray into public writing. Even as a child she had created books of imaginary heroes and heroines.[18] In her adult life, Eleanor continued as a crusader for causes she believed worthwhile, political opinions she thought were important, and social conditions that cried out for change. By the time of her *Reminiscences*, Eleanor had already written a full-length biography of her father, Rowland Hill, an article in a contemporary journal titled "Nova Scotia's Cry for Home Rule," and a discourse denouncing a would-be claimant to the development of penny postage.[19]

In her *Reminiscences*, as in all of her writing, Eleanor not only recorded her memories of the time, but also voiced her opinions regarding social conditions and attitudes. For example, she was revolted by the safety and sanitary conditions on board the Vanderbilt steamers and was not shy to say so in print. She was critical about situations such as this, which she viewed as inequitable; in this case, monopolistic business practices that impacted on the impoverished. This theme is repeated throughout her writings.

By the standard of her day, Eleanor had a markedly different view of the human species than many of her contemporaries. The average British colonist, whether a trader, missionary, government official or independent settler, viewed himself as culturally and morally superior to the Indigenous inhabitants, believing it Britain's right to subjugate, usurp land, take advantage in trade, and belittle artistic traditions and social systems.[20] This was the dominant attitude of the nations who forged colonial empires around the world, claiming distant lands and peoples as their property. Britain and Spain, particularly, claimed vast bodies of land and continents as their own. By establishing a military and governmental presence to legitimize their claims, the conquerors attempted to control the conquered and use the natural resources and wealth of the land for their own profit.

The written records of frontier women at times contain passages describing Indigenous peoples and exhibit fascinations for the perceived "oddities" of their culture, but accounts of relationships or even friendships between white people and non-white people are seldom included. In fact, there is almost a silence on the subject. For most colonists, First Nations people were separate and easily ignored, interacting only occasionally with the white immigrants, and then only within an economic transaction of some type. Clearly, there was little desire among many colonists to establish personal relationships, friendships or even civil communication with Indigenous people. In December 1862, the elected officials of the newly created City of Victoria passed a by-law "to take measures for improving the Sanitary conditions of the City of Victoria…" which made it unlawful for Indigenous women to live inside the city limits unless they were registered as servants.[21]

Eleanor, on the other hand, was interested in, and actively pursued relationships and even friendships with, the Indigenous and Chinese people[22] who populated her white middle-class existence. By today's standards and sensitivities, her writing may seem condescending at times, yet compared to the racist, vitriolic commentary of many of her peers, her openness appears quite enlightened.[23] The perspective of her commentary is often mixed—first complimentary, then critical— evidence of a dualism and a willingness to challenge stereotypes. For example, in one instance she describes Indigenous people, saying "their faces are as intelligent and prepossessing as are those of many among the best of my fellow-countrymen"; just pages later, recounting photographs shown to her by her Indigenous servant, she comments that they "were the most hideous I ever beheld" but to please her servant, she "feigned an admiration equal to her own."[24] In another example, she comments on Indigenous housing.

> On the new Reserve the tribe has built some good private residences and shops, and furnished them well; and most of the families are now sufficiently civilised to keep the buildings in a clean and healthy condition…. desirable as in some way these modern houses may be, they so entirely lack the unique picturesqueness of the older Indian lodge that one cannot help regretting the latter, which, though of the flat-roofed, square-box style of architecture, was redeemed from ugliness by a slight, but perceptible waviness of lines caused by its being built

not of mere squared logs but of by trees themselves barked and topped of their branches. Along its four sides stood at intervals stout, upright supports, some carved in more or less grotesque fashion, totems mostly. Windows there were none, but sufficient daylight entered through a doorway and the hole in the roof whence escaped the smoke from the central log-fire. Once inside the lodge, if a large one, the feeling suggested by the exterior view that its height was out of proportion to its goodly length and breadth was lost because in each corner lived a separate family or off-shoot of the parental family, whose belongings materially diminished the available space in the interior. Fairly comfortable seemed each corner, partially enclosed and lined as it was with the closely-woven mats of rush, etc., at which of yore the aborigines worked so patiently and well. Floor there was, of course, none, but the earth which did duty for one looked dry, powdery, and clean.

"Indian Village, Victoria Harbor, and Plan of Hut," ca. 1862–1866.
ARTIST: ELEANOR FELLOWS. B.C. ARCHIVES PDP00010.

Some twenty years later in wildest Donegal I saw many dwellings beside which the older style of Indian lodge here described would have compared favourably.[25]

Eleanor does not mince her words but boldly describes the downfall of Indigenous people as the fault of corrupt and immoral westerners whose trade in "firewater" was a "shameful business…so lucrative that the people engaged in it could easily afford to purchase the connivance of the police, one of whose duties, of course, was to aid the authorities in suppressing this very evil…."[26] "The story is a painful one…" she comments, adding: "Are my aboriginal friends 'the wretchedly degraded race' which unobservant people call them? If ever that reputation was deserved, upon whose shoulders should the blame be laid?"[27]

Other women whose diaries and letters exist write of the dirtiness of the native encampments and are contemptuous of a work ethic different from their own, and confident of the necessary civilizing force of their race to convert the "heathen masses."[28] Eleanor does none of this; in fact, for her time, she is boldly assertive in her belief that Indigenous people were wrongly categorized and views them as peers, intellectually and morally. A chapter from her *Reminiscences* titled "A House in the Woods" not only includes information on her activities and adventures, but illustrates how interrelated her life was with the lives of Indigenous people. It provides a unique view into colonial life. The chapter is included below.

The last year of my residence, half a century ago, in British Columbia saw us established in an old house built by the Hudson's Bay Company as a trading-post with the aborigines. It stood far up the Esquimalt Harbour, and close to a small peninsula[29] flanked on either side by a little bay, one a charming inlet shut in by thickly-growing shrubs, whence, at times, issued gaily-tinted humming birds of butterfly-like flight, which visited us fearless of harm because never molested, even entering the house, and settling for a brief space on some tall piece of furniture or other coign of 'vantage. This bay was carpeted with layers of smooth, cleanly-looking pebbles, so diminutive that to walk on them was as pleasant as if they had been sand. The other bay was a mere expanse of flat rocks with a muddy shore which even at low tide never seemed to dry.

View of Indigenous village, Victoria Harbour, 1870s.
PHOTOGRAPHER: JONES AND CO. B.C. ARCHIVES A-03443.

On the rock-strewn peninsula grew some giant pines[30] whose up-per branches in a gentle breeze gave out a pleasant, slumber-inviting sound, and in a tearing wind roared as loudly as the waves. And at the peninsula's extreme point, hard by where a sturdy cypress grew, lay one of those curious deposits of shells, bones, wood ashes, etc., relics of prehistoric times which are found in north-western Europe and other parts of the world, and are known as "kitchen middens." But vainly did I search for tokens of the long past in this deposit, only later to learn that it had already been often rifled, presumably by those among the officers of the Royal Naval Squadron lying in Esquimalt's outer harbour who had scientific tastes. Access to the spot was easy and the navy men often strolled along the track which went past our house, and sometimes dropped in for a chat and a little music.

From the front of the dwelling we had a grand view to southward of the mountains on the United States' mainland, the Olympian and Cascade ranges, whose summits are eternally snow-clad. This huge territory, extending far out of sight, eastward as well as southward, was the very substantial cause of that Vexed "Oregon question" regarding ownership which, ever and anon, came up for discussion in our British

Thetis Cottage, ca. 1920s.
UNIDENTIFIED PHOTOGRAPHER. B.C. ARCHIVES G-02416.

Parliament some three-quarters of a century ago. It was then an al-most unknown land whose great value, now so well understood, was not appreciated at the time; and thus we got rid of the troublesome thing in the same airy spirit of "Well, never mind; it's all in the family, you know!" with which we gave up a slice of New Brunswick and Quebec, the island of San Juan and sundry islets in the Gulf of Georgia, and the very many-miles-long coastline from Alaska south-ward which cuts off so much of north-west British Columbia from the sea.

A verandah bordered two sides of the house; and here I would often sit, and watch with interest those grand mountains with their varying aspects, now misty, intensely blue, and more remote than ever; now seemingly so near that, in spite of their very many miles of distance, one could descry, however faintly, their dark masses of dense forest and their sunlit vales and uplands. Curious was it also in summer to gaze at the thunderstorms raging about their flanks. The huddled rain-clouds looked so strangely diminutive and the vivid lightning-flashes so tiny, a couple of inches or so apparently in length, that one was reminded of the proverbial storm in a tea-cup. Of noise there was, of course, none audible.

The house was far from beautiful, but was substantially built of thick, squared logs, and was warm in winter and cool in summer. It had the small-paned windows peculiar to old-time colonial buildings when a breakage of glass was a serious matter. The rooms were lofty and of fair size, and the kitchen was vast. It was in this room that the aborigines used to bring their peltries and other things to barter against the Company's muskets, etc.,....[31] Overhead was an undivided attic, well-floored and roofed, and running the entire length of the house. It was the chosen and often noisy play-ground, especially at night, when high revels were occasionally held, of the rats who, of their own act, shared the dwelling with us, enjoying board and lodging free.

"View in Esquimault Harbor, looking South," 1866.
This pencil sketch by Eleanor Fellows shows their home Thetis Cottage on Dyke Point, as it overlooks Esquimalt Harbour. This sketch, and others illustrated in this chapter, were originally enclosed in letters sent back to family in England. Unfortunately the letters have not survived. ARTIST: ELEANOR FELLOWS. B.C. ARCHIVES PDP00008.

Not a rat was in the house when we took possession; but the very day of our arrival, we were assured by the young son of the nearest farmer from whom we were to be daily supplied with milk, that we might shortly expect the rodent invasion, as the animals always left the smaller house when the larger one became occupied. As the farm was at least a quarter of a mile away, quite out of sight, not even a chimney-pot visible, and only to be reached by a rough track over steep rocks and through dense forest, we felt sceptical as to the prediction; but our new friend was a true prophet. Now how did the cunning creatures find us out? Yet our experience was as nothing compared with that of other people if some of the stories told us were true. For instance, it was said by more than one eye-witness that when the gold-miners in goodly numbers went to a newly-found gold-field—their exodus being therefore a noticeable event—no matter how distant the place, the rats would be there as soon, or nearly as soon, as the men.

It was at this crisis that we took to sleeping with a loaded double-barrelled gun and loaded revolver between mattresses. Not that we feared attack from the adjacent indian village or from white marauders. We armed ourselves solely against the rats. Yet not for long. Familiarity, we know, breeds contempt. It sometimes also breeds a reluctant toleration. For presently I banished the fire-arms and the hostile attitude; and, as if by mutual consent, peace was established. The creatures were so clever and so amusing that I had not the heart to shoot them. When some toothsome morsel, saved over-night to re-appear at breakfast the following morning, was found to have disappeared during the night, no matter how carefully we had covered it, the theft had been so ingeniously effected that resentment changed to laughter. When the depredators nibbled little holes in the wooden partition-walls in order to effect surer entrance to the rooms, I simply stopped the holes with small squares of tin nailed across them; and went on stopping any freshly made. When at night I rose to attend to my children, the rats on the floor, table, or elsewhere regarded me with not unfriendly glances, and politely moved out of my way. I broke the peace-treaty on one occasion only, for the trodden worm will sometimes turn. One night I was roused from slumber by a vigorous scratching at my back. It was one of our self-invited rodent-guests plainly of opinion that I had monopolised more than my due share of bed, and bent on administering a rebuke. But even when I drove him away, he bore me no malice.

Of larger wild animals I never beheld one during our sojourn in that house, though pumas[32] were sometimes seen at no great distance; and til a very few years before wolves had been troublesome in the neighbourhood, and were still dreaded even on not far-off sheep-farms. Many a dolorous tale of their depredations did we hear from an old farmer who became friendly with us, and from whom we purchased meat, etc, and the mutton, as sheep, often dying a violent death at the jaws of their savage foes.

The rats, of course, we endured as best we could, but with the few human beings within reach we were on the pleasantest of terms. On our left, about a mile away along the shore, lay an Indian village;[33] and on our right, seemingly only a stone's throw across the water, rose

"The Indian Mode of Rocking the Baby," 1867.
Eleanor Fellows was fascinated by the Indigenous people who lived close to her on the shores of Esquimalt Harbour. Her sketches augmented the written descriptions in her letters. ARTIST: ELEANOR FELLOWS. B.C. ARCHIVES PDP00012.

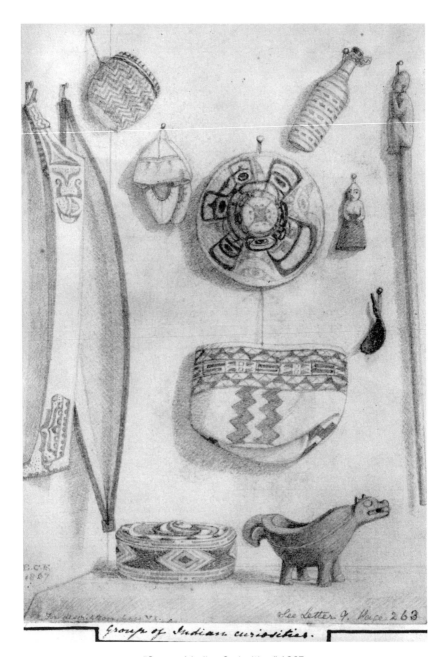

"Group of Indian Curiosities," 1867.
Woven baskets, hats, carved bowls and ornamental items decorated with Northwest
Coast designs were sold by Indigenous people to the white community, who collected
these "curiosities" for display or as gifts. ARTIST: ELEANOR FELLOWS. B.C. ARCHIVES PDP00011.

powder-magazine islet.[34] That it should be so near might have made me feel uneasy but that the custodian, whose house was also on the islet, was a steady, trustworthy man, who when one of our chimneys and some of the surrounding wooden tiles (called "shingles") were on fire, promptly came to our aid, and with the self-possession and handiness of the genuine old-timer, put out the blaze, and showed us how to act another time.

As for the Indians, I had now seen enough of them to take them at their true value. The "noble savage" is dead. Some people say he never lived; but that he was once an actual person I firmly believe; and I judge him partly by some of his race who are still living, but who have come little into contact with the white man. Therefore in the course of this chapter, and especially at its end, I hope to show that some of the ancestral good qualities still survive even among the aborigines who have come into that contact.

Before me as I write, hang portraits of three chiefs, men of to-day, but attired as were their forefathers previous to the coming of the people who call them savages—a term corrupted into the more modern "siwashes." The portraits are photographs; and photographs are truth-tellers. Man for man, their faces are as intelligent and as prepossessing as are those of many among the best of my fellow-countrymen. The three were not inhabitants of the neighbouring Indian village, nor did they live near it; but I mention them because their portraits serve as justification for what I say of them and of others among their kind. I may add that not a few of those British Columbian friends for whom we entertain the pleasantest recollection are of Indian as well as European descent.

That the aborigines of to-day are a "wretchedly degraded race," idle and thriftless, etc., is an accusation devoid of truth; and the lives of the villagers I came to know so well were proof of its unveracity. However early, on the long summer days, I might look across the broad waters of Esquimalt's inner-harbour, I never failed to see the canoes about in all directions and the day's fishing going steadily forward.

One very early morning I was startled to see, in the little bay whose mud never dries, some strange-looking figures which, at first glance, I took to be animals of, to me, a novel kind. They were Indian women bent double in their own peculiar way, each armed with a strong

"View in Esquimalt Harbor, looking West," 1865.
In this view, Eleanor Fellows has emphasized the isolated setting of Thetis Cottage.
ARTIST: ELEANOR FELLOWS. B.C. ARCHIVES PDP00009.

pointed stick, and using it to dig up clams. The clam lives in the mud, and at low tide sends up at intervals the funniest little fountain of water. The jet is only momentary. But it is sufficient to show the clam's whereabouts; the squaws go for him then and there, and speedily gather in a basketful.

Another early morning, when the tide was unusually low, and round about our favourite little bay, the star-fish of gorgeous colouring were left uncovered on the usually submerged rocks, a stalwart young Indian paddled his tiny canoe into their midst, and with unerring arrow, transfixed the exquisitely-tinted creatures one after another. As he needed both hands for his small bow, he laid his paddle aside, and, solely with the sway of his lithe frame, caused the canoe to bend to right or left, to dart in the required direction, to obey him like a living creature. It was a lesson in graceful athleticism.

With old John, as he was called, we had much to do. We employed him to chop the fallen trees into good-sized logs for our fires; and very well the work was done. But he had one failing, the result, perhaps, of constant early rising. There would be a cessation of the axe's sound which was replaced by one quite different. Guided by his stentorian snores to the spot where he was sleeping, I used, quite gently, to say "John," and in a moment he was wide awake. As a rule, the Indian is a light sleeper, a habit transmitted through many generations because of old he dwelt "in the midst of alarms." "Go on cutting the wood," I used to add in my best Chinook; and John, no whit offended at the interruption of his nap, went on till the next change of sound took place.

One early morning, I saw him in his canoe on the further side of the small peninsula, armed with a spear with which he perseveringly prodded the rocks a little below the surface of the water. What, I thought, could John be doing there? Presently, his task accomplished, he laid his spear aside, and, with both hands, pulled hard at something hidden in the recesses of a submerged rock. Out came at last a quivering jelly-like mass which, while its horrid-looking, but now harmless tentacles trailed in different directions, he lifted into his canoe. He had killed a large octopus—may I never see a more repulsive-looking creature!—with which, when safely stowed half in and half out of the canoe, he set off in the direction of his village. Just above those rocks I had often sat with my little ones about me.

On another occasion I saw John perform a really wonderful feat of seamanship. A sudden tempest had come on when he must have been far up the inner harbour, and before reaching home he had to cross a broad expanse of now angry waters. His canoe was small and unfit for stormy seas, but this was no paltry wood-cutting affair, and John was thoroughly wide awake. Bent nearly double, with head well down, he paddled at lightning speed, the canoe fast flying, yet threatening every moment to be swamped. I stood on the high bank close among the humming-birds-haunted bushes, and watched him breathlessly till he stood on shore, and dragged the canoe to safety.

The Indians used one paddle only, working it now on one side of the canoe, now on the other. It resembled nothing so much as a flattened note of exclamation turned upside down, and with a tendency to widen towards the middle of the blade.

Another friend was an extremely knowing old squaw, the most persistent, blandly-persuasive beggar I ever knew. She would sit on

"Very like my Lucy" is the caption on the reverse of this photograph,
which shows a young girl identified as "Tu·te·ma" from the Tseshaht band.
The handwriting on the caption is that of Eleanor Fellows.
PHOTOGRAPHER: CHARLES GENTILE. ROYAL B.C. MUSEUM PN04701A.

the kitchen floor, never on a chair, and, greetings over, would ask me for a little meat, because she was, oh, so very hungry. When sure of the meat, a bit of bread to eat with it was suggested; and so she would go on until she had collected the materials for quite a nice little meal, never asking for more than one thing at a time; and I, much amused, gave it as requested, to see when or at what her gently-voiced demands would cease. The comestibles secured, she would ask for a needle, then for a bit of cotton to thread it with, then for a piece of stuff to sew at, then for I know not how many more things, until at last I clapped my hands, and exclaimed, "hyack, clattawa!" which, being interpreted, meant "Be quick, and be off!" when she would vanish—til the next time. She was a curious-looking woman. In babyhood, while still bound to the board on which of yore Indian children passed their earliest infancy, not even legs or arms being at liberty, a large flat stone had been placed upon the upper part of her head, so that it should assume the long tapering shape which then was dear to aboriginal mothers. Later, a great walrus tooth had been permanently fastened into her chin; and with her face and the parting of her hair made as scarlet as paint could make them, she was not a little vain of her personal appearance, and doubtless, in her youth may have been considered a beauty.

But my chief friend from the village was Lucy,[35] a girl who, like her parents, had come under the influence of Bishop Demers[36]—of whom more anon—and his Catholic missionaries.

No walrus tooth in chin, no hideous malformation of cranium, no painted face had Lucy; and she was as good a girl, and as sweet-tempered, capable, and industrious as any maid could be. She used to paddle her small canoe across from the village, draw it up, and leave it on the pebbly shore, appearing at our door, punctuality personified.

Punctuality! Aye, trust an Indian to tell the time of day approximately at least, as well perhaps as did our own forebears ere artificial time-tellers were set up. Sun, moon, and stars were the Indian's guides, the best of clocks, too, never in need of winding up, of regulating, or of repairs in any way. Two artificial clocks had we, but the outdoor life, and the frequent rising in the night that were my lot taught me astronomy as I never before understood it, and made me thoroughly conversant with those phases of the moon whose meaning, simple as it is, I had hardly grasped till then. No wonder the Chinese, Chaldeans, and other nations whom we call semi-civilized were skilled astronomers. Had I continued to live in British Columbia and at the house in the woods, I too, with help of the celestial orbs, might have learned to read the time of day and night as easily as did my Indian friends.

Lucy was clever at washing the household linen, etc., at cleaning rooms, at doing many odd jobs which made her, very literally, a "help." Most amusing was it to witness her appreciation of civilised cookery. The first time she partook of cherry-pie was a record occasion; and I was careful that the treat should often occur again, for custom never staled her delight in it. One day, while busy with a large tub full of the household soiled linen, the poor girl severely scalded one of her arms. She was in dreadful pain, but I at once seized the flour-dredger, and powdered the hurt place liberally, the relief being instantaneous. The washing was laid aside, some tea, and a remnant of cherry-pie, happily discovered in the larder, were administered; and, later, she paddled her canoe home again, all smiles. Her gratitude knew no bounds. On her next visit she brought her chief household treasures to show me— the portraits of her family! It was still the era of the now forgotten daguerroeotypes,[37] hideous things which invariably made one's nearest and dearest folk look like the worst of malefactors; and Lucy's cherished specimens were the most hideous I ever beheld. One I especially remember. Half a century ago, the outer garment of every male Indian consisted of a blanket, fastened, in lieu of brooch, with a wooden skewer; and this particular one of Lucy's daguerreotypes showed a chief thus attired. The portraits were many, and the artist must have found the transaction profitable, for, in a spasm of generosity, he had gilded the skewer! The effect was most funny, but Lucy thought the adornment beautiful, and to please her I feigned an admiration equal to her own....

During my year's sojourn at this old Hudson's Bay Company's house I was twice shot at. The first assailant was a sailor from one of the men of war lying in the outer harbour. He was seemingly out for an afternoon of duck-shooting; and peppered me with small shot as I sat on the verandah with my boy-baby in my lap. I looked in the direction whence the firing came, beheld the man in his boat near one of the two small bays, and thought I had never seen a broader grin on any human countenance. Perceiving therefore that the incident was merely a blue-jacket's idea of a joke, I remained where I was, picked the shot out of my own clothing and the frills of the child's white summer frock, and when I looked round again sailor and boat were gone.

On the second occasion I was sitting in the same place, and again my little boy was sleeping on my knees. I was otherwise entirely alone, my old servant and twin daughters being out of sight and sound, wandering in the forest in search of wild strawberries and flowers. This time the shower of shot was nearer, sharper, more plentiful. Again I looked up, only to see a tall Indian, too tall to be one of our villagers, and to me a total stranger. He was standing, gun in hand, close to the short isthmus leading to the peninsula, not twenty yards away, and staring hard at me. Had I been new to the colony, and new to the aborigines, I should have been thoroughly scared. As it was I felt far from comfortable. The house was empty of human beings, and even the dogs had followed the wanderers to the woods. On every side the doors and windows were open, and should the man attack us, the child's and my chance of escape would be small. So, to quote a familiar French saying, I took my courage in both hands, and with the baby in my arms, sauntered leisurely down to where the stranger stood. In the Chinook tongue I hailed him amicably, asked what luck in hunting he had had, and chatted with him for a few minutes. He also talked in a friendly tone, but seemed unaccountably shy. Then I bade him farewell, and as leisurely sauntered to my seat again, but with the queerest sensation down my back—which in going from him I necessarily had to turn—wondering whether, ere I reached the chair, another volley of shot, this time perhaps striking a vulnerable place, might not be sent after me. But nothing happened; and when I turned to wave a hand in his direction, he and the deer which his gun had previously laid low were nowhere to be seen.

The man, not noticing my presence, and perhaps thinking the house unoccupied, as it often was, had doubtless fired at a bird or other animal near me, had missed his aim, and quite unintentionally bestowed the contents of his gun on me instead. His seeming shyness must have meant self-reproach mingled with relief at seeing that I chose to regard the incident as what it clearly was—an accident.

At no time during our twelve-months' stay at the house in the woods did the Indians of the neighbouring village act towards us in any hostile manner; and we lived near enough to be annoyed had annoyance been intended. Indeed, as I have shown, we practically sojourned in the midst of them; and the land all about the house and the waters round two sides of it were their daily resort.

One reason for this pleasant state of things probably was that the land on which the village stood had not yet become sufficiently valuable to tempt the white man's greed; and the aboriginal inhabitants were therefore let alone. Whether the near presence of the Royal Navy's men-of-war, or the many-years-long influence of the Roman Catholic missionaries kept the covetous away, and helped our Indian friends to remain self-respecting, I know not; but at the time we were their near neighbours they were certainly more happily circumstanced than the Songish[38] and other tribes who dwelt in the vicinity of Victoria, where as the little settlement of white men grew, and received immigrants who had no connection with the Hudson's Bay Company, there was much temptation to these later comers to get rid of the aborigines....[39]

Royal Navy vessels on the Pacific coast were stationed at Esquimalt Harbour at an area to the south of Thetis Cottage. Often many vessels could be seen anchored in the harbour. The building under construction on the right of this scene may be Thetis Cottage. Engraving published by the *Victoria Gazette*, July 1858.

Eleanor recalled her experiences with her hired help as "adventures." Unlike some other women in the colony,[40] she appears to have wanted to know about and to maintain relationships with Indigenous people hired as labourers, maids or nannies. The cultural mystique surrounding them, fuelled in part by scientific curiosity, contributed to this need. She also had Chinese "help." The following extracts reveal both Eleanor's ignorance of Chinese customs and a paternalistic attitude, but they are revealing in that she is willing to poke fun at herself, and at her ignorance.

Some anecdotes about old-time Chinamen servants come back to memory. A lady I knew in Victoria used to give dinner-parties on the model of those in the old country; or rather attempt to do so. The work of preparation was always tremendous, the consequent fatigue most wearing, the failures many, and sometimes ludicrous; and after the breakdown of her latest function of the sort, she wisely abandoned a practice which was entirely unsuited to a colony in its babyhood, rough to live in, and lacking nearly every mechanical contrivance that tends to labour-saving. Her Chinaman was a good cook, hard-working, and obliging, but possessed of a rather easily ruffled temper. An especially grand banquet was in progress at the lady's house, and the soup and fish courses had come to table, proved satisfactory, and been removed. Then ensued a long pause, so long that at last the hostess left her guests, and penetrated to the kitchen. The outer door was open, the stove-fire all but out, the place in confusion, the rest of the dinner only partially cooked, and rapidly cooling. Of John there was no trace, nor did he ever reappear. Something—no one knew what—must have offended him.

Another friend of mine possessed an unusually handsome grand piano, her pet piece of furniture. On one occasion she went to spend the day with her parents, but, before leaving, told the Chinaman to clean the house thoroughly, and set everything in order. On her return she was pleased to see that the place looked "as fresh as paint" but on entering her "best" room, she beheld him mounted on hands, knees, and even boots upon her cherished piano, his brush, pail, water, and other accessories of office beside him, and scrubbing at its polished surface as vigorously as if it had been a floor.

Yet another friend had often assured me that her Chinaman was a perfect treasure. He was little more than a boy, but wholly without silly boyish tricks, with a full-moon-like, amiable face, orderly ways, a love of toil, and devoted to her baby. One day, as she sat quietly sewing in the sitting-room, she heard in the adjoining kitchen a mysterious sound the like of which had never before come to her ears. She rose, gently opened the door, and peeped in. John, on hands and knees, with one arm was washing the floor, the other being clasped round the child, unto whom he was crooning some quaint Chinese lullaby, doubtless composed a few thousand years ago, the baby meanwhile at intervals crowing with delight. Un-willing to disturb the strange duet, my friend retired as quietly as she had entered. Alas, the treasure soon fell victim to the oft-recurring "gold-fever" epidemic; and to the de-spair of the house-mistress, departed to go north, and dig the precious metal at Cariboo.

A Chinaman at one time in my service covered the kitchen walls, doors, etc., very neatly with the local newspapers as fast as we had done with them. The walls being unplastered, thus showing the rough boards of which they were built, I rejoiced at John's evident sense of tidiness, never dreaming of what was to follow. When the paste dried he began to inscribe the sheets with large Chinese characters in some black pigment, causing the room to look like one of the usual large tea-chests, but with the outside inscriptions turned inside. Having no knowledge of the language, I was unable to decipher them; and my friends were equally at fault. Some surmised that John was an author of prose or poetry, and that, with a view to achieve immortality for his compositions, he resorted to this mode of advertisement. But a young English friend, much given to tease, suggested that, in order to en-lighten those of his own nationality and calling who should come after him, my Chinaman was recording in imperishable form his candid opinion of the household's mistress, and, with singular appositeness, doing so in the darkest of hues.

It is no longer possible for people of small means in British Co-lumbia to keep a Chinaman-servant, for of late years the powers that be have, in their unwisdom, levied a poll-tax of five hundred dollars (£100) on every "celestial" who enters the "country of the free." John of course does not really pay the fine; the actual victim is the householder, out of whose pocket a wage far heavier than he ever paid before is extracted. And thus many people are unable to enjoy the comfort afforded by possession of an often efficient and trustworthy "help."[41]

Letter writing was an activity in which Eleanor, like most young women of her age, was skilled. For a few years prior to her marriage, she had acted as private secretary to her father, responsible for generating and maintaining the voluminous correspondence of Rowland Hill in matters of postal reform and other business.[42] The letters she wrote to family members while in British Columbia were copious.[43] Filled with the details of daily living, friends, neighbours and local affairs, they were the only way she could communicate with her family in England and were no doubt a solace for homesickness. Eleanor's *Reminiscences* were based upon these letters.[44] The *Reminiscences* were structured as a series of vignettes, anecdotes and thematic commentary in which she discussed both the people and events of the colony.

The *Reminiscences* are important not only because they document Eleanor's thoughts, but also because they provide evidence for the activities, interests and preoccupations of white female society in the 1860s. It has been estimated that there were 100 white males for every white female in British Columbia in the mid 1860s.[45] Due to the scarceness of female population and the comparatively harsh living conditions, these women produced few written records that have survived through time, and those that have are generally just terse diary notations. By the 1880s, when women like Kate Woods and Violet Sillitoe were recording their experiences, life in British Columbia had dramatically changed. Transportation and communication were vastly improved, food and other supplies were in greater abundance and standards of living were much higher, yet even in 1881, at the time of the first Canadian census in B.C., there was a tremendous imbalance in the ratio of men to women in some parts of the province.

Eleanor herself was particularly well-known because of her musical talents. Articles in the *British Colonist* during 1864 record her involvement in concerts at both the Lyceum Hall and in private homes. Her training in the Italian operatic tradition, and willingness to perform publicly, made her an unusual commodity in days when women were subordinate to the public roles played by husbands and generally not encouraged to assume public activities. In this regard, Eleanor was unusual and may have deliberately pushed the boundaries of social etiquette. In 1864, at Mrs. Swainson Willis's Drawing-room Concert in the Lyceum Hall, Eleanor was listed on the program simply as "an amateur." She sang a solo ("Commee bello…from Lucretia Borgia") which was rendered "with the greatest taste, feeling, and power."[46] She was enthusiastically received. The following October she was described as "certainly the finest vocalist we have yet heard in Victoria, combining, as she does, a well cultivated musical taste, with a clear, rich, powerful voice, and an earnestness in her efforts which shows that she enters with the spirit as well as the understanding into the subject of the music…."[47] During the next two years, Eleanor sang publicly on several occasions, always eliciting positive and enthusiastic comments from local reporters: "her well trained voice enabling her to accomplish the difficult passages with ease;" "she displayed surprising command of voice and most skilled execution;" "the solo by Mrs. Arthur Fellows…was most sweetly and artistically sung, and rapturously encored."[48] She also sang at St. John's church, along with other talented amateurs such as "Father Brabant of the West Coast—a fine baritone, Mme. Beckingham, Miss Tissett"[49] and others. Eleanor's public performances separated her from the women of her class in colonial society. Whereas the latter were principally the audience, Eleanor participated in music concerts as a performer. Despite her prestigious background (daughter of Sir Rowland Hill) and wealthy upbringing, Eleanor was viewed by some of her peers as somewhat lacking in refinement. Rather than deferring to her husband in public and following rather than leading, Eleanor's strong personality overshadowed that of her husband. Compounding this situation, Eleanor's husband was in trade, and this reduced her social claim in the new colony. Her public performances placed her in the public eye and may have led to an increasing division between herself and members of the upper merchant and professional strata. Upper-middle-class Victorian attitudes to "the stage" and its performers are well documented in British history. It was acceptable for a woman to sing, play the piano or act among friends in a private situation such as a house party, but it was unacceptable for her to do so publicly upon a stage.

Additionally, Eleanor held less than conventional viewpoints on religion. Although raised in an Anglican family, and married at the Church of St. John, Hampstead, Eleanor had, by her own admission, a lack of orthodox faith.

> Among my many men friends, I have counted as some of the staunchest not a few priests of various denominations, men too broadminded as well as too courteous to make allusion to any lack on my part of orthodox faith. I may add that, on the other hand, I have always been free from that worship of the "black robe" which is supposed to be a peculiarity of my sex....[50]

Exposure to a variety of social reformers, educators, authors and politicians during her youth was no doubt responsible for broadening Eleanor's perspectives. In particular, Harriet Martineau, author of many discourses on social reform and a correspondent of Rowland Hill, seems to have been influential.[51] Martineau was raised as a Unitarian and during her lifetime variously embraced Roman Catholicism, eastern philosophy and atheism. She was often a visitor at the Hill family home.[52]

Although Victoria had a wide representation of Christian denominations, the majority of its leading citizens were Church of England and often not tolerant of other faiths or beliefs. This attitude was expressed by Jane Fawcett (whose husband, incidentally, was a distant cousin of Eleanor Fellows) and may have been shared by others in the community when she noted in a letter: "Mr. & Mrs. Fellows (the daughter of Sir Rowland Hill) I do not expect to derive pleasure from their acquaintance, this family connection of my dear husband…as I believe neither she, nor her husband have any experience of religion.—they are Unitarians—I believe that to be worse than Roman Catholicism...."[53]

Both Arthur and Eleanor appear to have made attempts to accommodate Victoria's social elite. Their first-born twins were christened at St. John's Anglican,[54] yet they also attended services at other churches. A friend, scientist and explorer, Robert Brown, recorded: "Met Mr. Arthur

Fellows & went with him and Mrs. Fellows to the Roman Catholic church." And on a later occasion, "Church (Hills) a Discourse on the Devil, at Mr. Arthur Fellows in the evening."[55]

Very little documentation exists concerning her social activities with friends, but what does exist leans more on the unorthodox than on the customary. Even in her *Reminiscences* she writes more of the friendships made among transients, young gold-seekers and adventurers than those with the established society-people who, by birth or economic status, were her social equals. She does not mention contemporary families such as the O'Reillys, Pembertons, Pearses or Woodses whose male heads of household were in governmental positions, nor the families of Victoria's merchants, the Roscoes, Rithets and Franklins, her husband's peers; nor, for that matter, even her husband's brother and his wife. She chose instead to tell us of the unconventional alliances, for instance, the friendships struck up with miners and transients.

> …they came in by thousands, from the uttermost ends of the earth, and in every variety of floating thing that could be relied on not to sink too easily. The mode of conveyance was necessarily limited because of land travel there was little or none. For in the Wild West at that distant time railways were non-existent, and the formidable "sea of mountains"—"twenty Switzerlands rolled into one" as the Canadians proudly call it—which barred access to those seldom-visited regions had not yet been explored, was indeed a veritable terra incognita….
>
> Of the gold fever of 1862 I was, however, an eye-witness so far as are concerned the landing and occasional sojourn of the newcomers at the port of Victoria. Cariboo, in which district the gold was chiefly found, I never saw, though by steamer and stage I have travelled a long way in its direction.
>
> It is an every-day saying that a gold excitement attracts the worst of life's failures, the world's riff-raff, the wiliest of rogues. The saying has only a modicum of truth. The crowd which in 1862 disembarked at Victoria or Esquimalt en route for the gold fields was composed in far greater proportion of those who, like our Norse ancestors, has [sic] in them the love of adventure and over-seas travel, or who, influenced by more modern views of life, believed their chances would be better

among a new than an old community. And with many of these I made friends....

In those days we were all young, enthusiastic, and firmly persuaded that we should speedily achieve fortune....

Three friends had before leaving England invented a fascinating costume in which to go out digging for gold at Cariboo. The costumes were all alike, made of some soft material and of rather light colour, prettily embroidered with narrow scarlet braid, decidedly becoming, and the very thing for a fancy ball. They were not donned till the wearers went on board the good steamer "Enterprise" bound for New Westminster, on the Fraser river, which port marked the end of the first and easiest stage of the long journey to the gold-fields. We went to the wharf to wish the three "good speed and good luck"; and I thought how much nicer they looked than the roughly-clad miners, some of whom were grinning widely for no reason apparent to ordinary onlookers. We never beheld those fascinating costumes again; and the three who had worn them avoided answering questions concerning their disappearance. Later we learnt from eyewitnesses of their brief existence that the fancy-ball garments had been discarded in a very few days as hopelessly soiled and worn out; and our friends, in due course, returned to Victoria habited much after the style of the miners whom perhaps they had hoped to teach how to dress suitably for the part to be enacted....

Many of our fellow British emigrant friends, recognising that gold-mining was hardly congenial employment, yet unwilling to return home in the character of unsuccessful members of society, wisely decided to remain in the young colony, accepting any sort of occupation they could find, and biding their time till they could do better, and perhaps some day set up a business of their own....

In the meantime, with an eye to economy, and it being the summer season—and in Vancouver Island the summer of 1862 was ideal— many lived in tents; and more than one pleasant little "Canvas-town" came into being, looking delightfully picturesque, especially at night, when the fires of pine branches and bracken were throwing out a cheerful blaze, and crackling for all they were worth. What jolly little impromptu meals were served up by very amateur cooks, what songs were sung, good stories told, and what a "high old time" altogether it was! Tea at Canvas-town was a sociable, refreshingly unconventional event at which we sometimes assisted, when, instead of Society small talk, we were regaled with the novel experience of our hosts....

As our friends got on in the world, they naturally took to dwelling in houses instead of tents; and with improvement in circumstances, pecuniary and social, there came ere long into vogue among us pleasant Saturday afternoon riding parties and unostentatious and thoroughly enjoyable picnics to favourite haunts in lovely scenery such as Sangster's Plains, Langford Lake, etc.... And the summer amusements alternated pleasantly with the winter ones such as dances, amateur theatricals, and concerts.[56]

The Fellows family was sociable with immigrants from other lands. "We knew Americans, Canadians, Germans, Italians, French and others, making little or no distinction of nationality but only of individuality; and it was from a German who in an earlier part of his life had sojourned in his native backwoods that I learned how to 'build' a log fire scientifically."[57] Undoubtedly Eleanor's ability with languages assisted her in socializing, but proudly asserting that it was a distinction of individuality, not nationality, that created her friendships is a very different standard than other British colonists of her day, many of whom stayed rigidly within the small hierarchy of their nationality and looked disdainfully at those of other races. In particular, the diaries and letters of Eleanor's colonial contemporaries, Sarah Crease, Caroline O'Reilly and Julia Trutch, reveal prejudice. In many instances they would not mix and saw no advantage in mixing with those of non-Anglo-Saxon backgrounds.[58]

Surviving photographs also provide evidence of the Fellows' unconventionality compared to their British counterparts. Only two photos of the family are extant. In my many years of research, only one portrait view of Eleanor alone, presented at the beginning of this section, has surfaced, and this is in an album compiled by an Anglican clergyman.[59]

Photo albums were popular in the mid-nineteenth century, and collecting the images of friends, family and famous personalities was standard practice. Many albums of photos compiled by colonial British Columbians include pages of photos depicting friends and acquaintances. These small photos, called cartes-de-visite, were exchanged and given away as remembrances to be added to albums. None of the many albums examined in the course of my research on colonial families contains an image of Eleanor or Arthur Fellows.[60] The albums contain images representing practically every other colonial family, and often images of people not resident in Victoria who may have just visited. This lack of documentation within the photo albums of the established families is also evidence of Eleanor's unpopularity.

If we examine the two extant photos of the Fellows family, again unconventionality presents itself. These images, seemingly the only photos from this time period, were donated to the Provincial Archives by Eleanor's children.[61] The groups in the photos include not only Eleanor, Arthur and their children, but various friends, neighbours and servants. The composition of the photos must be studied closely to discern who is who. These two photos are radically different from those documenting other colonial families. Photography was still relatively new and treated as a rather important undertaking by clients. Families commissioned formal family portraits or family groupings posed outside their residences, the family generally clustered around the front door and stairway and arranged in a manner that indicates familial connections. These photos were designed as statements of how the families wished to be presented; in addition to clearly stating the familial relationships, wealth and status were indicated by the residence itself.[62] This is not so with the Fellows images.

The first image shows the family in 1864 outside their home on Birdcage Walk. Arthur Fellows is shown holding one of the twin daughters and Eleanor stands beside him. On Eleanor's right is a servant who holds the other child. Their friend, the artist Frederick Whymper, is on the far left, and a neighbour's boy is on the far right. Anyone not familiar with the faces might be hard pressed to know which woman was Eleanor, as she is not holding a child, and one could even imagine that Whymper and the servant were a couple with a child. It has all the look of an outing and none of the look of a formal photograph.

The second photograph, from 1866, is even more casual and confusing. The setting is on the beach below the side verandah of Thetis Cottage. Both the seating arrangement of the family and the choice of

The Fellows family and friends outside their house on Birdcage Walk, Victoria, ca. 1863.
L TO R: artist Frederick Whymper; unidentified nanny holding one of the twin daughters,
Caroline Frances and Mary Clara; Eleanor; Arthur holding twin; young Walter Wilson.
PHOTOGRAPHER: CHARLES GENTILE. B.C. ARCHIVES A-02144.

location are odd. This image is taken not from the front door and steps, which would have been the more formal approach to the house, but below the side door. By their position on the beach, the people are not connected physically with the house. Sketches and photos of Thetis Cottage from other vantages show a more inspiring scene overlooking the harbour, with the snow-capped Olympic Mountains in the background. From the front steps, this view could be included in a photograph, so why did the Fellows family elect to be represented in such an inelegant manner?

The carte-de-visite format of the original print indicates that it was used and given out to friends, so they must have been pleased with the result. The Fellows were renting the cottage, therefore pride in ownership was not a motive in the photo composition, yet surely they must have

Fellows family at Thetis Cottage, Dyke Point, Esquimalt Harbour, ca. June 1866.
Nannies hold Arthur Jr. (baby) and son Rowland Hill; parents hold twins Caroline
Frances and Mary Clara; boy with dog is identified as Walter Wilson, a friend.
PHOTOGRAPHER: CHARLES GENTILE. B.C. ARCHIVES A-02145.

considered carefully the statement they were making through this image. If we examine the grouping itself, another unusual question arises. Which exactly is Eleanor Fellows? Three women are shown, each holding children. The woman on the left appears to be Indigenous, yet she is wearing a European-style gown; the other two women sit beside Arthur and each hold a child. Only because the other family photo exists are we able to determine that Eleanor is the woman seated on Arthur's left, holding one of the twin daughters. Presumably, then, the other two women are servants, but who is the young boy seated on the beach?

This is a confusing composition. Mother sits on a log with her face partly in shadow, father beside her on the beach with his legs straight out at the camera and soles of his shoes prominently displayed. Slightly behind and off to one side are two servants, formally positioned on chairs in the sand holding the youngest children, and closest to the camera, most visible in this small image, is an unrelated person.

This photo was sent back to England and distributed to family members who had not yet seen the children. No known studio group portraits were taken of the Fellows family in Victoria, so this and the earlier view on Birdcage Walk may have been their official photos. Unconventional—extremely so; other families dealt with the need to hold children differently. The separation between family and servants was clearer. These images, combined with commentary by contemporaries and the evidence of Eleanor's own writings, produce a profile of a rather unconventional, not wholly accepted couple.

Eleanor and her family remained in the colony only a short while. By 1868[63] they were in San Francisco, and the next year back in London. Plans were made to return, but they did not materialize,[64] although Eleanor and her children lived in Nova Scotia in 1882–83. By this time Arthur was estranged from the family and was elsewhere.[65] He did not figure prominently in the family life, and indeed, is never mentioned in Eleanor's writings.

It was not until 1909, at the age of 78, that Eleanor, accompanied by her daughters, revisited Victoria and found a much-changed town. The visit was an impetus to complete her *Reminiscences*, which she eventually published in 1916. She arrived as Mrs. Smyth, having remarried in 1903, and was socially received by families who remembered her. The Crease family, for one, was not impressed: "Callers all afternoon, among them a Mrs. Smythe [sic] and her daughters the Misses Fellows—not exciting."[66]

To the end, Eleanor remained a public personality. Although she maintained a large personal correspondence, she made many of her views and opinions quite public. In addition to her *Reminiscences*, she wrote letters to the San Francisco newspapers under the pen-name "Eve's Granddaughter," commenting on free trade.[67] She wrote a number of diverse articles and one major book. An article entitled "Nova Scotia's Cry for Home Rule" was written after her residence in that province. This was followed by a pamphlet, *Truth vs Fiction re: The Chalmer's Claim*, a rebuttal to those she believed were false claimants to the invention of the postage stamp. This pamphlet combined with "a few brief writings…in some of the later volumes of 'Notes and Queries' (and) sundry letters to the press"[68] all dealt with postal reform. Her greatest work, *Sir Rowland Hill: The Story of The Great Reform*, was published in 1907. At age 87 she completed *The Passing of the Penny Post* and, at age 93, *A Thirteenth Century Prophet and Some of His Contemporaries*, which in turn was followed by *An Essay on Chaucer*. Unfortunately, Eleanor's visual records were not as lasting. Apart from her pencil and watercolour sketches of Victoria, only one other work is known to exist.[69]

Eleanor remained active and vocal throughout the last years of her life. As noted by her daughter Caroline, "she at length passed peacefully away on December 31st, 1926, within three months of completing her 96th year."[70]

NOTES

1 Sir Leslie Stephen and Sir Sidney Lee, eds, *Dictionary of National Biography* (London: Oxford University Press, 1917) pp. 867–871.

2 Eleanor took lessons from artist and teacher James Matthews Leigh (1808–1860).

3 Eleanor C. Smyth, *Sir Rowland Hill: The Story of a Great Reform* (London: Fisher Unwin, 1907), p. 41.

4 The marriage took place on 15 October 1861 at the Parish Church, Hampstead. General Register Office, London.

5 *Victoria Gazette*, 21 June 1859; *New Westminster Times*, 18 February and 3 March 1860.

6 Matthew Macfie, *Vancouver Island and British Columbia* (London: Longman, Green, 1865), p. 65.

7 Eleanor C. Smyth, *An Octogenarian's Reminiscences* (Letchworth: private publication, 1916), p. 54.

8 Ibid., pp. 54, 59–63.

9 Victoria *Daily Chronicle*, 6 January 1862.

10 *Reminiscences*, p. 71.

11 "List of persons liable to pay taxes." *British Colonist*, 3 August 1862.

12 *British Colonist*, 17 February 1862.

13 *British Colonist*, 31 July 1863.

14 *British Colonist*, 1 July 1864.

15 *British Colonist*, 3 April 1865 and 2 April 1866.

16 Only portions of these chapters are included here.

17 *An Octogenarian's Reminiscences*, p. 9.

18 *The Brazen Horseman*, written in 1845 and privately printed (typeset and illustrated by Eleanor, her brother and sister) the following year, is in the collection of the British Library.

19 Only eight publications have been located to date. Others were undoubtedly written and will surface in time. As Eleanor Fellows, she published "Nova Scotia's Cry for Home Rule," *The Nineteenth Century* (Condon: Kegan, Paul, Trenen and Co., 1886) and *Truth vs Fiction, re: The Chalmers' Claim* (London: R. Forder, February 1892); as Eleanor C. Smyth, *A Thirteenth Century Prophet and Some of His Contemporaries* (Bexhill on Sea: private publication, August 1923); *An Essay on Chaucer* (Bexhill on

Sea: private publication, April 1924); *An Octogenarian's Reminiscences* (Letchworth: private publication, 1916); *The Passing of the Penny Post* (London: private publication, July 1918); *Sir Rowland Hill: The Story of a Great Reform* (London: Fisher Unwin, 1907). Eleanor (as did many women of her time) wrote under pen-names. This makes it difficult to locate other writings. One known example is a series of letters to the editors of several San Francisco newspapers signed "Eve's Granddaughter." Unfortunately, further publications have not yet been located.

20 There are several articles on this topic; for B.C., most notably Myra Rutherdale "Revisiting Colonization through Gender: Anglican Missionary Women in the Pacific Northwest and the Arctic, 1860–1945," *B.C. Studies* (Vancouver: University of British Columbia Press, Winter 1994).

21 Cited in Peter Baskerville, *Beyond the Island: An Illustrated History of Victoria* (Burlington: Windsor Publications Ltd., 1986), p. 44.

22 The first Chinese immigrants, an estimated 4,000, arrived in 1860 to work in the gold fields. Subsequently many returned to Victoria and found jobs in service. Baskerville, p. 44.

23 "The natives are hideously ugly and atrociously dirty: their customs are beastly, manners they have none...." Edmund Hope Verney to Sir Harry Verney. See Allan Pritchard, ed., *Vancouver Island Letters of Edmund Hope Verney, 1862–65* (Vancouver: University of British Columbia Press, 1996).

24 *Reminiscences*, p. 92, 96.

25 Ibid., pp. 101–102.

26 Ibid., p. 98.

27 Ibid., pp. 98, 102.

28 See records of Sarah Crease, Caroline O'Reilly, and Julia Trutch, B.C. Archives.

29 Dyke Point on Esquimalt Harbour.

30 All conifers were regarded as pines by British immigrants. She is actually referring to the Douglas-fir.

31 Thetis Cottage and 64 acres of land were owned by Capt. James Cooper, former H.B.C. employee. Although no corroborating evidence has been located, it appears that Cooper may have traded with the Indigenous people from this building. See Maureen Duffus, *Craigflower Country* (Victoria: self-published, 1993) for further information on Cooper.

32 Cougars were often referred to as pumas in nineteenth-century B.C.

33 This is the area now known as Maple Bank.

34 Cole Island, some 400 feet long and 200 feet wide, was named in 1846 for a master on HMS *Fisgard*. It served as an ammunition depot from 1859–1938. It is now a federal historic site. Duffus, p. 37.

35 Lucy has been identified by photo-historian Carole Williams as Tu-te-ma from the Tseshaht Nation.

36 Modeste Demers (1809–1871) was consecrated Roman Catholic Bishop of Vancouver Island in 1847.

37 Daguerreotypes were the product of an early photographic process in which pictures were made on light-sensitive, silver-coated metal plates.

38 The Songhees band, which initially moved close to Fort Victoria in 1843 to have the advantage of trade, was subsequently twice displaced from their village sites in the inner harbour, first, to allow construction of the Birdcages, and second, as the city expanded across the harbour to Victoria West.

39 *Reminscences*, pp. 89–98.

40 Sarah Crease arrived in 1858 and lived in Victoria and New Westminster over the years. With a young and growing family she was always in a state about servants, or lack thereof. Rather than hiring Indigenous people, she preferred hiring white or Chinese women, whom she thought more easily trained. See Kathryn Bridge, *Henry & Self: The Private Life of Sarah Crease, 1826–1922* (Victoria: Sono Nis Press, 1996; Royal BC Museum, 2019).

41 *Reminiscences*, pp. 76–78.

42 This was a job she re-commenced after her return to England and continued up to her father's death in 1879. See *Sir Rowland Hill: The Story of the Great Reform*.

43 Unfortunately none survive, but sketches inserted in the letters have survived with annotations indicating their relationship to the text. For instance, one sketch reads: "See letter 12, page 348." B.C. Archives PDP00008.

44 Arthur Fellows Jr. to N. De Bertrand Lugrin, n.d. (ca. 1927), Arthur Fellows Papers, Bruce Castle Museum, Tottenham.

45 Cited in Adele Perry, "'I'm So Sick of the Faces of Men': Gender Imbalance, Race, Sexuality and Sociality in Nineteenth Century B.C." *B.C. Studies* (Vancouver: University of British Columbia Press, Spring/Summer 1995).

46 *British Colonist*, 26 July 1864.

47 *British Colonist*, 27 October 1864.

48 *British Colonist*, 26 July 1864; 27 October 1864; 20 April 1864.

49 Edgar Fawcett, *Some Reminiscences of Old Victoria* (Toronto: W. Briggs, 1912), p. 122.

50 *Reminiscences*, pp. 116–117.

51 *Sir Rowland Hill, The Story of the Great Reform*, p. 131. For biographical information on Martineau see *Dictionary of National Biography*, volume 12.

52 Her niece ventured to Victoria, where she resided with Eleanor's sister-in-law during the 1870s.

53 Jane Fawcettt to Emma Wignall, 1862 extract, Fawcett Family Collection, B.C. Archives.

54 Record of Baptism, 1863, St. John's, Victoria.

55 Robert Brown, Diary, 11 December 1864 and 17 January 1865, B.C. Archives.

56 *Reminiscences*, pp. 80, 83, 85–87.

57 Ibid., p. 87.

58 See Crease and O'Reilly family correspondences and diaries, various dates, various family members, B.C. Archives.

59 The album, compiled by Rev. Robert J. Dundas, is in private hands in England. The portrait of Eleanor Fellows contained in the album is reproduced here with kind permission.

60 A very few contain portraits of Alfred and Louisa Fellows, who undoubtedly remained in Victoria longer. Louisa ran a private school that made her image popular with students whose family albums contain portraits identified only as Mr. or Mrs. A. Fellows. This led to some detective work to ascertain that none was Eleanor or Arthur.

61 There is no reference to further photographs in the correspondence between Nora de B. Lugrin and Caroline Fellows at the time of Lugrin's research for *Pioneer Women of Vancouver Island, 1843–1866* (Victoria: The Women's Canadian Club, 1928). No reference exists either in correspondence between Arthur Fellows Jr. and Mrs. Cree of the Provincial Archives during the 1930s, or in the collections of the B.C. Archives or Bruce Castle Museum.

62 Kathryn Bridge, *Two Victorian Gentlewomen in the Colonies of Vancouver Island and British Columbia: Eleanor Hill Fellows and Sarah Lindley Crease*, unpublished M.A. thesis, University of Victoria, 1984.

63 The family sailed from Victoria in June 1866 for San Francisco and may have revisited over the next couple of years.

64 Robert Brown to Eleanor C. Fellows, 24 January 1870 (B.C. Archives), discusses the Fellows family plans to go to "the Far West" again.

65 Perhaps San Francisco. Arthur's years beyond those in B.C. are a mystery. He did not die in England, nor did he leave an estate.

66 Josephine Crease, Diary, 4 November 1909, B.C. Archives.

67 The identity of Eve's Granddaughter was revealed in a letter to the editor of the *British Colonist*, Victoria, 10 August 1878 from Arthur Fellows.

68 Eleanor C. Smyth to L.V. Morten, 24 December 1907. Arthur Fellows (Jr.) Collection, Bruce Castle Museum.

69 Oil painting of a young woman and a punt along a river, collection of the author.

70 Caroline F. Fellows, quoted in *Pioneer Women of Vancouver Island*, p. 215.

HELEN KATE
woods

1854–1937

Kate Woods as a young woman, about the time she journeyed to the Nass and Skeena Rivers, ca. 1880. PHOTOGRAPHER: UNKNOWN. PRIVATE COLLECTION.

HELEN KATE WOODS came to British Columbia at the age of 11. The circumstances of her arrival were rather unusual. She was born in Ireland in January 1854, the youngest daughter of Richard and Anne Woods.[1] For reasons not recorded, Richard Woods decided to emigrate to Vancouver Island and did so in 1861, accompanied by his wife, two eldest daughters and infant son. The two youngest daughters, Kate and Emily, were left behind in the care of aunts. Years later, Kate recalled:

> Being left behind in the old family home in Ireland was a heartbreak for two little girls of seven and eight, but as the years rolled by was perhaps an advantage, because impressions are more deeply imprinted after seven years of age, and therefore memory stowed away so many mental pictures and recollections of the old land and the leisurely life we lived there. We were left in the care of two devoted aunts and were happy and well cared for, and as I looked back many a time in a mood of comparison, we were so well off. The old family home was so well established, and the dear aunts were busy and occupied in various ways about the place; but I had never seen real "work" done by anyone but servants. Stiff crinoline of heavy silks and such materials were worn, and fine hand-made laces and fischus…. Even little girls, as I looked back many times, wore fine clothes.[2]

Eventually Kate and Emily were summoned to join their family in Victoria. The problem of who would accompany them on the long journey was conveniently solved because Bishop George Hills[3] with his new wife was returning to the colony after a leave in England. The Bishop lived in Victoria and administered the diocese of British Columbia, which included parishes on Vancouver Island and the mainland, for the Church of England. The Woods family were parishioners at St. John's in Victoria, and Kate's uncle, the Rev. Charles T. Woods,[4] ran the Boys' Collegiate

School in Victoria, under the auspices of the Church of England. These connections allowed the Woods to be comfortable in knowing that the girls were in good care on the journey.

Well, after four years the day came when my sister and I were ready and packed, to take the long trip to Victoria, British Columbia. Right Rev. Bishop Hills had been at home for a visit and was returning with his bride and very kindly was to take charge of us on the journey. Naturally the aunts took advantage of the opportunity to help the colonial family here, and prepared cases of useful presents as well as many photographs for us to take along.

We left Ireland just after Christmas—the voyage to Victoria taking just over two and a half months. Childlike, we were all set to enjoy every minute of the great adventure—unfortunately the first part of the Atlantic Ocean was never visible to us as we immediately were afflicted with sea-sickness! However, by the time we reached Colon on the Isthmus of Panama, we considered ourselves good sailors.

We crossed the Isthmus on a little railway train; in retrospect it seems it was not much larger than the original street-cars which we were to enjoy in Victoria many, many years later. Everything tropical interested us greatly—the beautiful flowers, huge trees of oleander blossoms, the fiery flamboyant trees, poinsettias and hibiscus in ever so many bright hues. Large tree ferns bordered the roads, their tall fronds meeting overhead. Wild fruits, oranges, bananas, limes, and of course coconuts in abundance, were a delight to us. The natives fascinated us, as also did the little chameleons which were friendly enough to attend all our outdoor meals gathering crumbs.

The next chapter of our journey took us from Panama to San Francisco and it seemed we no sooner became accustomed to our second steamer than we transferred to a third one, the *Sierra Nevada*, which was to take us all the rest of the way right into Esquimalt Harbor. This piece of the journey was also interesting, but by this time we two little girls were getting weary of the long voyage, but as we neared our destination our excitement ran high.

The arrival of the *Sierra Nevada* was quite an event, apparently, in the lives of the colonists in and around Victoria. Naturally, in those early days passage by sea was the only travel to and from San Francisco and therefore the mails were heavy also.

As we came up the Strait of Juan de Fuca on March 10 and around Race Rocks, we got our first view of the land which was to be our home and Esquimalt Harbor…which had been surprised with a heavy fall of snow. In those early days all navigation docked at Esquimalt, Victoria having no docking facilities…. Well at last our ship was alongside, and to our surprise we found the snow ten inches deep. Even in those long ago days we were assured that this weather was most unusual for March! Very soon we were received by our parents and sisters, and I shall never forget the surprise—and I suppose, shock—I received, contrasting their appearance with the relatives at home in Ireland. They had been here four years then, and naturally were now a very "homespun" colonial family—no silks, no laces, no finery at all. A pair of my little brother's heavy boots had been brought along for me to wear, knowing that my pretty shoes would not be suitable, especially in the snow; and this, for all the kind thought prompting the action was about the finishing touch to what I later admitted was an 11-year-old's pride.

However, greetings continued and then we all climbed into a "Democrat" and began the drive to town. We left the conveyance somewhere near where the Point Ellice bridge crosses the Arm, and continued by water to "Wood's Point" where the homestead, "Garbally" (Irish for home-on-hill) was established.[5]

In spite of the culture shock, it was not long until Kate and her sister settled into the new family relationship and the routine of pioneer life.

Garbally was a country home, modest in size, with cultivated vegetable and kitchen gardens, berries, grapes and fruit trees. The land extended from what is now Gorge Road to the ocean and north to the vicinity of today's trestle over Victoria Arm.[6] There was no road through the property; the closest was Saanich Road (now Douglas Street), which ran on the eastern edge, but it was little more than a trail.[7] The Woods family possessed a cow and chickens. As in other families, the children played an active part in sharing indoor and outdoor chores.

The daughters attended Angela College, the Anglican girls' school,[8] and did very well academically, especially in the arts.[9] Both Kate and her sister Emily were talented at sketching and watercolours, winning numerous prizes. The school on Burdett Street was several miles from

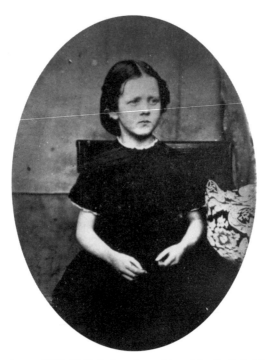

Kate Woods, ca. 1860–1862, before she and her sister Emily left Ireland to join their family in Victoria. Daguerreotype. PRIVATE COLLECTION.

Garbally, the Woods' family home on Victoria Arm, ca. 1870s. Pencil sketch by Kate's sister Emily Henrietta Woods. B.C. ARCHIVES PDP01605.

Garbally, but such a distance was not considered an impediment, and Kate and her sisters accompanied their father, who, as Registrar of the Supreme Court, also travelled daily into Victoria. They left Garbally by boat, rowing toward town, around Point Ellice, until they came to Rock Bay and then walked the rest of the way.

In 1868 there was much excitement in the Woods family. Kate's eldest sister, Alice, was to be married to Robert Tomlinson. Tomlinson was a young missionary who had stayed with Kate's uncle and his family the previous year before heading north to the village of Metlakatla, where he joined William Duncan of the Church Missionary Society. Tomlinson and Alice fell in love, but as she was very young and Tomlinson was committed to this north coast posting, they were told to wait a year until Tomlinson's return to Victoria.[10]

The marriage took place at St. John's Church on 24 April 1868, with Dean Edward Cridge officiating.[11] Four days later, Alice and her new husband, accompanied by seven Nisga'a men and one Nisga'a woman, left in canoes, departing from the Hudson's Bay Company wharf (now the foot of Fort Street). They travelled out of the inner harbour, around Clover Point[12] and up along the east coast of Vancouver Island and then north along the coast to Metlakatla and Kincolith. The trip was 24 days in duration.[13]

The story of their courtship and marriage is a romantic one; the reality, though, is more sobering. Alice was 17 when she married and left her family and a comfortable middle-class existence in Victoria. It was to be several years before she would again see her family. Her life was changed forever. She was one of the very first white women to live amongst the Nisga'a, Tsimshian and Gitxsan people. By necessity she quickly adapted to this new life, becoming fluent in the Nisga'a tongue and assuming different and demanding domestic duties and responsibilities.

Twelve years later, in April 1880, 26-year-old Kate Woods and her brother Edward, aged 21, sailed north from Victoria on board the SS *Otter*. Their destination was the small Indigenous settlement of Kincolith, on the Nass River. This was to be the embarkation point for an exciting overland journey to Ankihtlast,[14] a tiny mission on the Skeena River, near Kispiox. Here, Alice and husband, Robert Tomlinson, lived with their children, having moved from Kincolith in 1878.

Alice Tomlinson had just given birth to her fifth child when Kate set out to visit. The family had seen her only twice since her marriage: once in July 1871, when she came to Victoria anticipating a difficult birth (this second child, a daughter, died shortly after birth),[15] and once again in the winter of 1877, when the entire Tomlinson family came to Victoria.[16] At this time, when the Tomlinsons returned to Kincolith, Kate's younger brother Edward accompanied them. It seemed he too wished to become a missionary. Edward was of great assistance the next year when they undertook the arduous trek over the grease trail from the Nass to the Kispiox River to establish the new mission at Ankihtlast.[17] Alice became ill from typhoid while on the trek and nearly died. She took many months to recover. The following year, Edward returned to Victoria, ostensibly to re-acquaint himself with the young woman who was soon to become his wife,[18] but also to persuade Kate to come back with him to Ankihtlast. Edward knew the life Alice led, and the loneliness. He was also fearful for her physical condition, as her growing family was a handful and she was pregnant again.

The eldest Tomlinson child, Robert Jr., was born in 1870, his sisters in 1872 and 1874, and a baby boy in early 1878. Robert Jr. was capable of much help with the farm and other chores, though he was still young. It could not have been easy to raise a family amid the many respon-sibilities of the mission. Often Robert Sr. had to be away from the mis-sion—sometimes for several months at a time—visiting and counselling parishioners in a variety of villages and camps. Evenings were taken with prayer meetings, gardens required tending, farm animals had to be fed and cared for, and bread had to be baked and food prepared for the family. As well, the Indigenous people living at the mission were to be trained and taught domestic duties, carpentry and other skills. It was an exhausting regime. Coping with another birth and an infant while juggling these varied tasks and caring for the other children was not a situation to which Alice was looking forward. The closest white woman was some distance away,[19] and even though several Indigenous families lived at the mission, Alice craved the companionship of her sister and the company she would provide in this isolated settlement. Edward would bring Kate with him on the journey. It was a perfect opportunity.

Kate's decision to undertake this trip was guided no doubt by her desire to see her sister, and by the situation of Alice's pregnancy. But added to these familial reasons for a visit was another, somewhat mysterious reason, hinted at in the beginning pages of Kate's own journal, which she kept on the trip. Here she wrote: "I need not enter into any of the causes which induced me to undertake the trip…." These tantalizing lines suggest perhaps some inner turmoil, perhaps an affair of the heart which would make necessary a change of scene and routine.[20] Indeed, as Kate stayed with her sister until the fall of 1881, a long visit of almost 18 months,[21] we can perhaps suppose a need for time and distance from Victoria.

Leaving Victoria on 3 April, the *Otter* travelled up the coast, arriving in Kincolith on the tenth. Here Kate and Edward disembarked and were met by Henry Schutt and his wife, missionaries for the Church Missionary Society at Kincolith.[22] After a rest, provisioning and consultations with many residents concerning their proposed route and timing, the two left Kincolith on 13 April, in company with Nisga'a guides.[23] The trip was on foot up the Nass and then overland, following traditional grease trails up through the mountains, to Ankihtlast on the Kispiox River near its confluence with the Skeena, a travelling time of 26 days. In April the winter snows were deep, necessitating travel by sleigh and snowshoe. It was, without a doubt, a very different experience for city-bred Kate. Living in Victoria, snow was, at most, an inconvenience for several days. It was not a situation in which much travel was undertaken, but rather a time for retreating indoors. The sheer physical energy necessary to travel each day was unprecedented in her personal experience. The demands were unusual and at times placed her in physical peril. Yet, reading her journal,[24] she appears exhilarated, re-living each treacherous situation and the daily struggles and revelling in the sheer novelty of it all.

Her journal is intimate, and her frequently inelegant style adds to her colourful writing. Here, Kate recorded the daily events and managed to sketch with a pencil some of the surrounding landscape. The following is a transcript of the complete journal as it exists today.[25] Unfortunately several of the early pages dealing with her arrival on the Nass are lost, and the journal ends rather abruptly after their arrival.

Kincolith, where Robert and Alice Tomlinson lived for nine years before moving up the Nass to Giltlakdamiks and then to Gitxsan territory, at Ankihtlast on the Kispiox River.
PHOTOGRAPHER: MISS COLLISON. ROYAL B.C. MUSEUM PN11428.

3 APRIL 1880

A bright pleasant April morning. The wind blowing gently, the sea shining brightly, and the Hudson's Bay Company's Steamer *Otter*, lying in the harbour of Victoria, Vancouver Island (lat 48.20N) with steam up ready to start on a trading trip along the North West Coast to the mouth of the Naas River (about 55 North lat.). I am a passenger on board, intending in company with my brother to leave the steamer at Kincolith, a village at the mouth of the Naas, and make my way inland to where my married sister is living at An-Kiht-last (55.3– N. Lat 127.30 West long) not far from Kish-pi-oux or what is locally known as "the forks of the Skeena."

I need not enter into any of the causes which induced me to undertake the trip, but I think that the leading events of the trip are worth recording, and so I proceed to set them down from my diary.

Leaving Victoria on April 3rd we reached Kincolith on the 10th. The journey so far was uneventful, and this our real point of departure.

The SS *Otter* at Victoria, 1880s. Kate and Edward Woods travelled on the *Otter* up the coast to Kincolith.
PHOTOGRAPHER: UNKNOWN. B.C. ARCHIVES A-00104.

Croisdaile's salmon cannery on the Nass River, 1882.
PHOTOGRAPHER: UNKNOWN. B.C. ARCHIVES B-03546.

Oolichan (eulachon) fishing on the Nass at Kincolith, 1884. Note pile of oolichan on ice
behind dog sled. PHOTOGRAPHER: UNKNOWN. B.C. ARCHIVES D-03105.

Processing oolichan at Fishery Bay, ca. 1884.
PHOTOGRAPHER: UNKNOWN. B.C. ARCHIVES C-07437.

13 APRIL TUESDAY

In the morning of this day man after man came into Mr. Schutt's room and came over to have his say as to the advisability of our going up the river. Some said wait for a week for then all the ice will be gone. Others said "Please yourself" and after a conference of about an hour they all came to the conclusion that if we must go we might as well start at 2 o'clock. They wanted to wait a week for all the ice would be gone. [T]he river is free below the fishery and again 3 or 4 miles above & there is a band of ice across the river stretching for about 5 miles. When it was settled we should go, we got everything together ready for starting then we got as warm as we could & had some hot coffee. Mrs. Schutt was most kind she gave us a quantity of bread cakes and pies to save us the trouble of cooking bread for a few days. After many delays we started from Kincolith at 1/2 past 2. Victoria time. Mr. & Mrs. Schutt, Sissy and the 3 girls came down to see us off.

People came out of their houses as we passed to send their "toiks"[26] to Mrs. Tomlinson. They all wondered very much at my "strong heart" in undertaking such a journey. The wind was blowing very hard when we left against us & till about 5 it was very rough indeed only for the cold it would have been very pleasant. We managed to keep tolerably warm. Edward & Arthur shot sea gulls…after a good deal of loitering we came in sight of the ice about 7:30. Arthur had left his sleigh there but when we looked for it, it was gone & could not be found. We were in a dilemma & Arthur very woebegone but it could not be helped so we went on and presently saw on the bank a sleigh it was not Arthur's they landed & took it on board. We told him it was not right to take another man's sleigh even if his was gone but greatly to our relief we found he only wanted to take the loan of it for we could not get over the ice without it. He said he would return it in the morning so we were content. A few more minutes brought us to the ice where we all landed. The men took everything out of the canoe first and put…all in a pile and lifted the canoe on to the sleigh and cached it firmly on then put everything back again into the canoe, we were ready to start. E[dward] & I started to walk in front but Arthur called us back & told us we must walk by the canoe and hold it all the way for the ice was unsafe. Then if we came to a hole or the ice gave way or that we come to a hole we would be safe. This was pleasant intelligence to say the least of it. Arthur went first with his arm over the bow pulling & guiding. I came next grabbing on with all my might especially when the ice felt soft and plashy. E came next about the middle of the canoe, first one side and then the other. Liggy-you-en and Heat-ckq pushed together at the stern and we started. In some places the ice was lik ice, smooth and slippery, but these places were few and far between; mostly it was soft, plashy, thawy, snow stuff. We sank sometimes five or six inches in the so-called ice. Oh the wetness of it! Oh the dampness thereof! It was not unlike a Victoria thaw after a heavy fall of snow.

After about one hour a "Smell" stole slowly, gently—not sweetly—over our senses. It could not be compared to roses on a May morning nor did the perfume suggest eau-de-cologne. Stronger and more refreshing it grew at every step, it was invigorating! We pressed forward, eager to reach the fountain spring of this sweet perfume, we knew we were nearing shore, for the smell was nothing more or less than fish—eulachen remains and grease. I never did so heartily appreciate a bad smell for I knew our journey must be nearly over! We could see the lights of the houses on before us and they really looked very pretty, the bright fire lights shining through door-ways and walls. It was now quite dark only the whiteness of the snow gave light for there was no stars and no moon. We left the canoe near one of the huts and then Edward and I walked up to the fishery while the men carried up our packs. We got in by some back way but a white man came out when the dogs barked and showed us a light. We asked for Mr. Nice[27] (Mr. Croasdaile's[28] head man at the fishery and one of our fellow passengers of the *Otter*). After waiting a moment he got a lantern & showed us the way. We found Mr. Nice in the best room at the fishery & he very kindly offered us his room. The room was about as big as E's room at Garbally—about as long but wider. In it were 2 beds, a table, a book shelf minus the books and a chair (I nearly forgot it) and last but not least a stove. It looked as if the stove must have come out of the Ark but really I saw the date 1860 on the front. There was a fire enough on to roast an ox. We were not at all cold by that time our walk had made us quite warm. Mr. N offered to go & see if he could get us anything to eat but we told him we had lots of provisions. He wished us goodnight & left us to our own devices. We were hungry for since we left Kincolith we had eaten nothing but some cakes Mrs. Schutt gave us. We made tea & had some of Lillie's[29] potted beef which is first-rate. (By the way all the food made of the split peas turned out a complete failure the tinned peas mushy & the peas pudding fermented, so we took a bag of oatmeal from Kincolith instead.) It was past 11 when our tea was over so we turned in as quickly as possible. I used my own blankets for the first time, E used Mr. Nice's.

And now a word about our crew. Arthur is the head man, the canoe belongs to him & he is the sense of the party. He speaks very good English & knows all we say though he likes to talk Nishka best.[30] The boy Heat-ckq (pronounce the first part of his name Heat all e same Hot then draw in your breath in almost a hiccough). He has another name Sansanah but we generally by way of a change and for short call him "Gum-boots" for his weak point is his boots of which he is very proud. They are long gum boots up to his waist. The top generally when not in use turned down in graceful fold. Whenever we came to a shallow place out he jumps & pulls us through. He giggles at every joke that others make. He is from Kincolith and knows a little English. The other is the clown of the party his name is Liggy You-en[31] (pronounce as spelled) he makes jokes & cuts capers and plays tricks on the others. He is from the Skeena his great amusement is to learn English and spell every new word he hears. He knows English letters but very few words. He is great fun. He breaks forth in song every now & again then makes believe to be so tired he can work no more, he is very amusing.

WEDNESDAY 14 APRIL.

We got up at half past 6 and were not quite dressed when Mr. Nice announced that breakfast was ready. He waited for us outside the door & escorted us to the breakfast room (it is in another house) where we breakfasted. First I must tell of the party. Mr. Nice our host, his friend Bob[32] by name (he was also a fellow passenger on the *Otter*). We could not find out his other name—he is a German or Prussian, and a Scotchman named Matheson.[33] They were very kind & hospitable. The room we breakfasted in was bedroom, kitchen & sitting room in one & they were their own cooks. Breakfast was porridge first for all who wished for it in a huge milk can, the vessel in which it was cooked. They did not call it porridge but "Mush" then small fish fresh & fried potatoes, hot rolls, bread, coffee and last but certainly not least in point of quantity a china washing basin of boiled dried apples & peaches mixed.

After many delays Arthur looking for his sleigh and found it far out etc. etc. We started about 10:30. All the things packed again & this time the canoe was put on the sleighs (Edward bought one for $2 to expedite matters) one was set mid near the bow the other near the stern. Mr. Matheson came to help us start & put cross pieces on the sleighs under the canoe to steady her then off we started. Mr. N ran down to say a last goodbye and off we went. The ice seemed even worse than what we had crossed the night before and Edward took 2 more men on to give a hand—Patrick & Thomas from Kincolith. We had not gone 100 yards when the man at the bow gave a shout and a jump & the ice broke under his feet & he went through. I was quite close to him holding on to the canoe. Edward was a yard or so behind me & he shouted to me to come back which I did very quickly. I did not get in the hole but the water splashed back over my feet & on to my dress. An Indian woman Catherine[34] from Kincolith came to help but when the sleigh slipped into the hole I thought it very advisable to run to the shore & we took hands & jumped from block to block till we reached the shore. There was no real danger I believe except in getting wet. The ice is 4 or 5 or 6 feet thick (except in the holes & cracks) and the blocks in general rest on the earth below. There was a great commotion then to haul the canoe and sleigh out as the bow was in they had to haul it out backwards & the ice we had passed was nearly as bad or worse than at the bow. They no sooner got it out at the bow than the stern sleigh and all went into another hole. Edward went in one leg at this break. This was not a very reassuring way of beginning our day's journey, but it was the only serious adventure we had. Catherine & I remained near the bank while the others adjusted the canoe & started afresh. The ice got better as we went on & soon we walked again by the side.

We saw some strange sights. I should like to have taken sketches but of course sketching was out of the question. We met a canoe coming down on the ice they had one sleigh under the middle and as they were coming <u>with</u> the wind they had a sail up. Two men & a woman ran along beside but the wind & the sail did a good share in the work. We were facing the wind and it was blowing hard. We saw several old crones at work drawing their sleighs some full some empty going for and returning with their fish or grease. In one place we met a sleigh piled up with boxes & bundles and on the top of all sat an indian lady by no means a slight party either & in her hand she held a pole with an old black petticoat fixed on for a sail. Her husband ran beside holding a rope that was fastened on behind & so they actually sailed along the ice.

The wind was blowing, as mother would say "enough to shave a mouse". After going along for a mile or more, Arthur called out to us to come to the canoe again (we had left it for better ice nearer shore) when Catherine & I came over he told me to get into the canoe so E helped me in & piled me up with the tent etc to keep me warm and so I rode as in a carriage with my back to the wind it was famous.

Thomas and Patrick went at the bow, Liggy You-en on the side, Heat-ckq on the other near the front. Catherine at my side & E on the other & Arthur at the stern sometimes. The procession moved slowly when the ice was bad but sometimes they all ran off at a good trot. One time they were dragging along rather slowly when they came to a good piece of ice when Arthur shouted out "Get up old hoss" and Liggy [Y]ou-en (the clown) screamed out "Git up Sally" and with that they all went off full tear, jumping, running & shouting & didn't we fly along over the ice. It was grand fun. They put the snow shoes standing upwards in the canoe just at my back and over that Arthur put his best coat to keep the wind off. It was very snug. I had a drive nearly to the end of the ice, 3 miles I should think. We passed Kitaux [Gitiks] on the ice. We met some people then too with their sleighs. The ladies dress, or rather the elderly ladies dresses are useful if not ornamental. They all, or a great number wear blanket leggings, but the old ladies look first rate. First their feet are encased in moccasins which are very clumsy, then blanket leggings fitting nearly tight, then a blanket skirt reaching only to the knee, some a little longer, a blanket jacket made of all manner of patches (their blanket clothes are made

Greenville on the Nass River, 1881.
PHOTOGRAPHER: EDWARD DOSSETTER. B.C. ARCHIVES B-03577.

from the pieces that are given away at the giving of property & so they are made of all sorts of pieces). Then outside of all either a blanket shawl or a robe of fur, skinny side out & the hairy side in like Danny O'Flynn, and hats or hoods close fitting made of blanket after this style.

We reached the end of the ice at 1:30 where the wind was blowing very hard, too hard to have lunch out of doors so we went into one of the Indian houses and made our tea and had our meal. The indian houses…but of them we became better acquainted later on. After lunch we canoed till 7:30 and then camped. The ground was covered with 2 ft of snow, crisp & dry. They cleared the snow away to put the tent, the men put up their sail & made a fire between the sail & tent then spread dry branches on the cleared ground and we all lay or sat with our toes up to the fire & got our meal ready. We had tea, potted beef, cranberry pies and buns that Mrs. S. gave us. This was my first camping out and it was not under the most favourable circumstances, the place was ugly but we made the best of it.

15 APRIL

We left our camping ground at 8:15 and off again. The Naas River is altogether very much smaller, narrower and more insignificant than I had imagined. Canoeing began to be very interesting and in some places exciting for the water was very shallow and tremendously swift in places. As Edward expressed it we were going very fast by water though very slowly by land, that is the water was rushing past at a most tremendous pace, so we looked to be going very fast but by land at times we scarcely seemed to move we were going so slow at times. LiggyYou-en & sometimes Heat-ckq & sometimes E to help them would get out to tow the canoe. They walked on the snow on the bank, and sometimes the river ran like a gorge and it took all their might to paddle & to pole up. It was very exciting at times and I enjoyed it very much. We stopped to cook lunch & to make a good fire for E was very wet, for every now & then the ice they walked on would give way & they would go in up to their knees. At evening it became very cold & looked like snow (it had been snowing on and off just a few flakes during the day) and we were drawing near to Kitwin shilk [Gitwinshilk, also known as Canyon City].

So we asked Arthur if there was a good camping ground before we reached the village. He said we had better go on to the village and stop there as he was afraid it was going to snow and for Sig-it-tum-ha-nah's sake (or Siq-ittum-nab, "The Lady") it would be better to be under a roof, so I thought we could not refuse. So on we went. It was fearfully cold. We soon reached the village about 7:30. Arthur went up first and chose a house for us to stay in. All our traps were carried up. The hostess placed 2 stools near the fire for us & we sat down. We prepared our meal as quickly as we could for we were rather afraid of being invited to partake of a meal. The inmates of the house were numerous though Arthur said he would choose a large house with few people, so that we should have lots of room. First there was an old old man quite blind. I fancy he was the grandfather of the family. Then there was an old old women, the grandmother, she appeared deaf for most of the time she shouted[35]....At first I felt highly disgusted at every thing I saw but I thought the best thing would be not to see more than I could help & to look on the best side (if best side there was which appeared doubtful at first) but there was plenty of warmth, fire, <u>air</u> and <u>no bad smells</u>. I began to wonder what the folks at home would think if they could only see us then and there. To prevent the ashes falling on my head I made a cap (like Mr. Morley taught us) of one of Edward's red handkerchiefs & wore it all the evening which I am sure added greatly to my personal appearance. E looks so much at home wherever he turns up it surprises me. He looks just as much at his ease sitting at an indian fire or making bread in the back woods. He does most of the cooking, I lay the table, that is, put all we are going to eat out on a mat while he prepares the meal. He does not seem to mind getting nearly roasted over the fire & I do very much indeed. We had prayers about 10 that night. Arthur read out of his bible & had prayers in Nishka. The night before we had it in English (all except the hymns) but that night in the Indian house there were so many that could understand Nishka we asked Arthur to have prayers. (He had been a teacher for a long time) We sing "Tum ama dalactum" (Glory to Thee my God)[36] every night. We turned in about 10:30 and slept soundly though our surroundings were strange to say the least of it. Soon snoring was heard on all sides & all were fast asleep.

16 APRIL, FRIDAY

We left Kit-win-shilk at 7:30 & canoed on, scenery, river etc very much the same only more narrow, more swift, more difficult. We got at midday to I-a-nish [Aiyansh] where we landed and had lunch. There were no indians here. This is only a small village.[37] All Christians. This is the place where Robert built the school & Arthur was sent by the Kincolith people to be the teacher. After lunch we had a long delay in mending Edward's sleigh which had been broken on the ice. We reached Kit-lak-da-mich [Gitlakdamiks] about 2:30 where Arthur told us that if he could find a man to take his place he would not go on the trail with us for his feet were sore. He hurt his left foot some time ago in playing foot-ball. He found a boy from the Skeena "Yack'o dades" by name, pronounced very much like "Jack of Spades." "Dades" he is called. He joined us and on we went. E and Dades on landing at the ice (for we came to where the river was all frozen over again and we had to get out) fell through. E got one leg wet, Dades two. They were both soaking so we thought it best to stay for the night though it was still quite early only about 4 o'clock. The fire was lit & they changed their clothes and we had a meal. After tea they played tricks (the cup of water on the back of their heads to pick something from the ground, tying their wrists together with rope etc, etc, etc.) They were very clever at the tricks and knew some very good ones. We said prayers about 10 & then to bed. A very pretty place this time & an old camp which made it all the better. The Chinee (as the Chinamen are called) camped there a few nights before so there were lots of branches ready cut for beds & lots of fire wood.[38]

17 APRIL, SATURDAY

Left our camp at 7:30. Were all up at 5:30, had breakfast and all started walking on the ice. Arthur came with us for about 1/2 mile & then bid us good bye and went back. On we went & in an hour reached the end of the walk on the ice & the head of navigation & the beginning of the trail. The trail is covered with from 2 to 3 feet of snow in general, in some places where it was drifted it appears as much as 6 or 7 or 8. The morning was very cold & fresh so the trail was very hard & crisp and dry. We stopped a great many times to rest, lit a fire at mid day & had a meal. Walked on again, E & L going first. We knew the trail, though it looked as much <u>unlike</u> a trail as could well be imagined, by the tracks the Chinese had made before us. They appear to have worn snow shoes, all but one man & he wore boots and went through the snow at nearly every step, in some places he must have gone through to the very top of his leg. At first it was a great nuisance for we had to look at the trail all the time or we would have fallen if we had got into his holes, but afterwards we felt thankful for the track for we would not have known the way without his big tracks acted as a guide along the way.

The sun was intensely hot and about 2 o'clock the snow was so soft we all got out our moccasins and snow shoes. It took a long time to get them all ready and started again. Off we went. Heat-ckq (or Sansanah as the others always call him so I shall call him by that name) drew the sleigh with his pack on it, on the level ground or down hill he had a very easy time but going up it was fearfully hard for him. LiggyYou-en and Dades carried their packs on their backs poor fellows they did seem loaded. E had his pack his gun & my bag all on his back. He would not let me carry any thing. So off we trudged sometimes on the top of mountains sometimes in valleys. I saw the first good place after 4 o'clock I would like to stop but we did not come to water till 5. There we stopped on the top of a little hill with lots of pine trees all round and water about 50 yards off. Snow shoeing I did not find hard work. Not nearly so hard as I had heard it would be. It took 2 hours before we began to get a meal ready for first we cleared enough space to put the tent. We chose a spot that had once been used for a camp before for we could see the poles that had been used for the [sail?]. The snow was about 3 ft deep, we cleared it away with snow shoes for shovels and in clearing E found an instrument made of silver we both think it is a medical instrument of some sort. It is like a syringe. The boys had to get plenty of wood as it was Saturday night and E made bread after tea in preparation for Sunday. We went to bed about 9:30 tired out. It was freezing lik.

SUNDAY APRIL 18

We got up very late for there was no hurry as we were going to remain in camp all day. By late I mean about 8 o'clock. We had breakfast and cleared away in a leisurely manner. The fire had gradually descended during the night as it thawed through the snow and now it was on terra firma and we were seated all round at an elevation of about 3 feet. E would call it "downstairs" and invited me several times to come downstairs. The cooking was all done "downstairs" but we lived upstairs except if our feet were cold, then we sat upstairs and hung them down into the lower regions. It looked very strange to see the way it had gone down, the snow all round did not thaw only for the space in which the fire was built, about 6 x 5. We could not move at all outside camp without snow shoes as the snow was very soft & we sank in it if we tried. About 11 we had service or rather prayers. E read part of one of the gospels, then we sang a hymn in English (Heat-ckq knew a great many we only knew <u>one</u> in Nishka & that is an evening hymn). After dinner about 1, E and I went for a walk. We did not go far as in every direction it seemed up hill & up hill if very steep is rather hard work in snow shoes. The camping ground this time was in a very pretty place. In a thick wood of hemlock, balsam, birch & pitch pine. Most of the afternoon the men sang hymns & mostly in English…Heat-ckq acting as teacher. They have splendid voices and strange to say sing in part without ever having learnt. Their voices blend together beautifully. When we came back from our walk Heat-ckq taught me a Nishka hymn one which I admired very much with he and Liggy You-en's help I wrote it out as it sounded, and we afterwards sung it at evening prayer. The rest of the day was spent in looking about and taking things easy which we all deemed very well able to do and enjoyed it very much. I think when people are on a trail it would be a very good plan to have 2 Sundays in the week, both half days instead of one whole day once a week. We went to bed about 10 our usual time. Oh, I nearly forgot, we had marmalade for a treat & enjoyed it immensely & thanked JA.[39]

MONDAY APRIL 19

We were up at 5:30 but did not leave camp till 8. There was so much to be done we made a splendid tramp in the morning for the snow was so dry and hard & we made spendid time. We took lots of rests & so did not feel tired. Stopped at midday & had lunch in the afternoon. We passed a place called Kit an gelk [Gitwinshilk], reached a good camping ground…& so pitched our tent for the night…. We had a delicious treat for supper fresh meat, that is tinned venison which Mr. Nice gave me the morning we left the fishery.

TUESDAY 20 APRIL

We had intended to be very early in starting this morning but one thing and another delayed us and we did not get off till 7:45. E & I started first but after we had gone about a mile E said he was afraid we were on the wrong trail as it seemed to go down to the river (Naas) so we waited till the others came up and then we found that we were right. In winter weather the trail goes for a long way <u>on</u> the river but in summer it goes a long way from the bank. We went down a gentle incline and were soon <u>on</u> the Naas river. At this place it is about 150 yards wide from bank to bank. The ice covered it at each side but in the middle it was open for about 15 or 20 yards, rushing, roaring, twinkling down over rocks & ice and making a great roar. We got on the ice and walked for about an hour when we came to a place where the river was sound all the way across. We saw a camp fire on the far bank, our men shouted & we soon heard answering shouts and in a few minutes 2 Indian women made their appearance on the ice at the other side. We all sat down to have a rest while they came across to call. One wore snow shoes the other had bare feet. They belonged to a hunting party. They stood and talked for some time telling and hearing all the news. They said the ice was good for a long way so we could walk on the river. Our men then went across to the camp to get some dried salmon and we went on slowly. About 12 [o'clock] our men caught up to us and a fire was lit and we had a long rest and lunch. The banks on each side were nearly as steep as a hill & in some places the top overhung the lower part. After lunch we started off again still on the ice and when we had gone about 2 minutes we had to sit down and put on our snowshoes for we went through about 8 inches at every step. We got along better for a time but soon the ice got so bad we had to go one by one. Dades went out on the river first the river just here takes a turn round a sharp point of rock and…very swiftly. The ice was gone in the strong part of the stream and at the sides it was a good deal broken up. Dades with some difficulty got to the point of the rock and sat down to wait: when he saw us coming he called out to us, we could not quite make out what he wanted so E took me to a place of safety standing on a rock on the bank while he went to explore. After about 5 minutes he came back & told me to come. We had to go one by one for the ice was so bad & in some places there was a little water over the ice when we got to the point we had to climb up on the bank. Off went our snow shoes & we all walked in moccasins, if <u>walking</u> it could be called. This is somewhat the shape of the river or rivers for it was where the Anhaun [Cranberry River] joined the Naas the meeting of the water made so swift a current that the ice was so bad. The lines

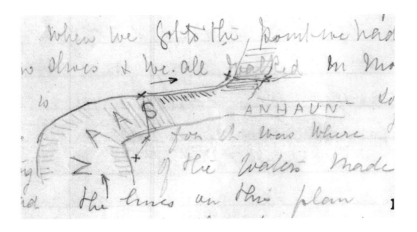

on the plan represent the ice, the arrow represents the direction we were going, the x shows where we landed, first to cross the point, then on with our snow shoes and across the river one at a time, then on the bank on the far side, then we had to cross the river again, and this time it was very exciting work for the ice was worse than ever here. The water was running 4 or 5 inches in a swift current <u>over</u> the ice in the middle of the stream. Dades went first E next then I came & then our other 2 men all in a string with a long space between each and we had to wear the snow shoes for they helped to spread our weight over a larger surface. So we all had to go one after the other there was nothing for it. It felt so strange to be walking on ice through a very swift current for the current caught one's snow shoes at every step but it was safer than without. We reached the bank in safety and then began to ascend. It was very steep & the snow soft and bad, up up up we went, walking, resting & toiling for half an hour. In some places it was so steep that E & I came to the conclusion that it was 67 degrees. My necktie was very much in my way for several times I stood on the end of it. E said he thought it was only a wonder I did not stand on my hair. In one place it was so steep and difficult that we only made 150 yards in actual distance in 40 minutes and working all our might all that time. Oh it was weary work. It was nearly [4?] o'clock when we reached the top. We walked on for about an hour sometimes up sometimes down but could find no water. We were all tired so we said we must stop. Branches were soon chopped for beds, trees cut for fire. (They always cut down trees for the fire, they generally chose dead ones as they are much drier than fallen timber. They think nothing of chopping down one 14 inches in diameter.) Liggy You-en took the gun on the way & shot a nice fat grouse which we had for tea, it was so delicious. When we stopped for the night, he took the gun again & just as we had finished tea he brought in another. We had our feet wet all the afternoon and it felt so delicious and strange to say going through the Naas river did not feel cold in the least. We did enjoy our supper immensely. I don't know why but every thing one eats or drinks does seem so good. The tea always seems as if there never was such tea and the pallid meat and the dried apples and even the rice and bread as seem so good. E spoils me the whole time. I never do a thing when we get to camp while things are getting ready all I have to do is to sit down or lie down and rest.

"Luandalahau River...Indian bridge...," 1880.
Pencil sketch by Helen Kate Woods. B.C. ARCHIVES PDP01698.

E and I have found out that <u>all</u> proverbs are <u>not</u> true. We have proved that. The one about not being able to cross a bridge before you come to it is a complete failure. A mistake in fact, for the Anhaun river, the one which had to be crossed on an indian bridge, everyone told us the bridge was broken with the snow this winter. So how to pass it we did not know. We thought we would wait till we came to it & then see what could be done and how we had crossed the Anhaun or rather crossed the Naas above the Anhaun so we had really crossed the bridge before we came to it.

WEDNESDAY 21 APRIL

We left our camp very late at 9 o'clock and had some hard snow shoe-ing all the morning for we had no trail for the first hour or two. For in crossing the Naas as we did, we did not reach the trail until we had gone some miles. We had lunch about 1 and then our toil commenced in real earnest. If we thought this hard work in the morning, it was

"Near Salmon House, Anhaun River, April 22, 1880." Below the sketch, Kate
Woods has written: "This large cage is let-down with the open side down
stream. The salmon going up get into the cage & cannot get out, then the man
goes out on the sticks and draws up the cage & takes out his salmon."
Pencil sketch by Helen Kate Woods. B.C. ARCHIVES PDP01696.

doubly hard in the afternoon. We took off our snow shoes and walked in moccasins. The trail was mostly clear from snow, so most of the time we walked on ground but such ground over logs through birch & hazel nut groves, thick thick groves too and sometimes in rough streams which really felt very cool and pleasant, and sometimes through thawed snow in which we sank to our knees at every step. The country looked not unlike a burnt hill side at New Westminster for all the trees of any size had been burnt & the hill was covered with an undergrowth of small saplings. On and on we went without taking a rest all the afternoon and camped about 5, really tired out and so sun burnt. The sun was very hot but not so hot as on Saturday.

THURSDAY 22 APRIL

We were up very early [at] 5:30 and had breakfast and left camp at 7. The walking was splendid for a time as the snow was dry and crisp & we walked in moccasins. It froze very hard in the night, the blankets got quite wet round one's mouth with the frost. We got along famously for the walking was so easy. I like walking in moccasins if the road is walkable at all. One's feet feel so cool. We reached the salmon house at 8:30 but every one was away. After looking about for some little time we saw a pack on the ground so we knew there must be some one about. The boys went down to the river to see if they could get some fresh salmon and came running back to ask me to come down to see them catch the fish. We went down to the river and there saw the man that owned the pack. He was catching salmon in a sort of a large cage or trap. It was made after the style of a mouse trap. It was a huge wicker basket in the shape of a cup but at one end the wicker work was made inside in shape of a point & this end was put down the stream. It was then sunk in a very swift place & the salmon going up the stream trying to get up the falls ran into the trap but could not get out as all the points of the wicker work poked inwards. When the salmon got in the basket is lifted up out of the water & the man went out on a kind of platform made out over the river and hooked the salmon out one by one through a hole in the top of the trap. He took three out while we were there. I took a sketch of this place it was so pretty. We saw several graves round the salmon house, all made in the shape of little houses. One very strange one was like a little house only all the lower part was a sort of lattice work. All the top closed except on the side. We looked in and saw as it were on a shelf the figure of a woman sitting, the head and hands were carved with care and she was dressed in good & nearly new clothes. Her skirt was new blanket blue & a jacket of red cotton & a handkerchief on her head and ear rings in her ears. The head was nearly life size. By her side was a box about a yard long. E thinks that the bones of the dead were in it and I suppose that this was intended to represent the woman whose grave it was. While we were waiting & resting there at the house a girl and 3 children came up and presently a woman they were all on their way down the trail. These were apparently the wife and children of the man we met first. We gave the woman some thread & the children some chocolate which they seemed to appreciate very much. We put our snow shoes on directly we left the salmon house for the county was open, the snow was soft. Got along very well till lunch time. We stopped quite close to an indian camp on the trail where Edward bought some "Mi" and some "ish".⁴⁰ The party consisted of a man a woman & 2 children. They came over to make an acquaintance. They were on their way down the trail, they had come from Kitwanskole [Kitwancool]. We then saw a very tiny pair of snow shoes, the smallest I had seen, home manufacture, they belonged to a little boy. They were about 6 or 7 inches wide and about 16 or 18 inches long. They all wear snow shoes (all that are able to walk have to wear them). The indians told us that the trail farther on was very bad with logs and water & that we might have to leave it & go through the woods to the left which we did but it was fearful through streams over logs, some of them so much as 6 feet from the ground & covered with 2 feet of snow on the top. Snow shoeing all the way. Oh it was frightful work, for a long way it led through a swamp. E says he thinks now that we would be able to climb a tree in snow shoes and I really believe we could. We got on the trail again about 4 o'clock and camped about 5:30 in a little ravine facing a glorious snow capped mountain not unlike Mount Baker.

FRIDAY 23 APRIL

We left camp at 8 and as it had been freezing hard in the night we went along smoothly in moccasins for about an hour then rather heavy snow shoeing over bleak hill sides. The others did not catch up to us till we stopped for lunch, they were having an extra good breakfast as they had fresh salmon & grease. Liggy You-en brought in two the night before, he gave them both to us but we thought that was rather hard on them so we gave them one. The road in the early afternoon was heavy but not very bad. Soon we reached the Anhaun again & scrambled along its bank for a time then across a large swamp. This brought us to the foot of the mountain. From the foot to the top it is 5 miles. E said in summer it could be walked in 2 hours and a half. It was then 4:30, we knew we could not get to the top for the trail was so bad but we thought in an hour and a half we could get half way or more so we started. We could not follow the trail, it was so bad, so Liggy You-en[41] went first and we followed. Everything was covered in snow so it was impossible to see the exact way. I never in all my life did such walking. We got completely out of our course and the snow was worse than it had been before, oh infinitely worse, sometimes in sheer despair we took our snow shoes off. If only there was a clear patch on a hill side but we thought it took too long a time & we were as wet as we could be so we got them on and kept them all the rest of the way, over streams on trees and through streams with the ice cold water up to our ankles but there was no other way and oh they did feel cold. But it grew worse and worse, the snow was so soft that snow shoes and all we sank 2, 4, 5 or more inches at every step. It was a weariness even to drag & lift ones feet and all up hill, we toiled on till 7. I never did such walking and don't want ever again to do anything like it. E said he never knew snow shoeing so bad, if he had only known that the trail was so bad he would never have taken me. At 7:30 we stopped but Sansanah and Dades did not arrive till about 3 quarters of an hour after us. We were all tired out and it was so late & so soon got dark everything was most uncomfortable. Oh I nearly forgot to write about one treat that we had on Thursday evening and that was the "ish" that Edward had bought. After tea "Sansanah" took some "ish" and some water in one of our tin basins and beat them together into a froth with his hand until it was all a mass of frothing bubbling pinkish brown stuff then we ate it in true indian style that is we all dipped our spoons into the basin while he kept stirring. E made 2 little spoons of wood for himself and me. Dades took a large spoon but the boy that was making it did not need a spoon for he licked his hand as he stirred beginning at his wrist and ending at the tips of his fingers. The other boy did not have any he does not like it. It has to be eaten while being stirred. A little of it I found very satisfying. We put lots of sugar in, the berries have a sort of taste sweet, creamy & velvety at first but bitter like quinnine I think one would like them very well if one got them often & got over the objection to the style of eating it. I often find myself doing things most extraordinary such as eating "ish", things I would have been horrified at before. I now quite understand what used to puzzle me before that after years of teaching and civilizing the indians do not seem to care to think it worth the trouble to keep themselves or their children or houses clean or neat for they live in such a free and easy style every one doing what he or she thinks fit, eating, drinking, sleeping, going and coming, when, how & where they like. It must be so much easier just each one to suit themselves. In their houses they seem to have no prepared meals. A pot of food is boiled either potatoes or fish or anything. When it is cooked anyone standing near takes it off the fire then any one that wants to eat, eats. Others that don't feel inclined to, visit or lounge round or go to sleep and whenever they have nothing else to do they lounge about in their blankets. Even these boys that are with us do the same when we get into camp and the work is done. They sit and lie about in their blankets, boots and stockings off and while one boy cooks the others lie on the ground and take little sleeps (that is if there is no mending to be done) sometimes the camp in the evening is a busy scene. When we come in, all round the fire on branches or sticks pointing up for the purpose hang stockings, moccasins, blanket shoes, & strips of blanket, and rags, of all descriptions. I've got 1 pair leggings, 1 pair stockings, 1 pair blanket shoes, 1 pair of cloth shoes, 1 pair of moccasins and all these have to be dried regularly every night. Every one else wears as much or more not counting the leggings. Then all round the camp are seen the snow-shoes 5 pair standing upwards in the snow, the points are just poked into the snow & they stand up right all round. Then after supper is over, all the snow shoes that have been broken during the day (for the lacing often wants mending) and all the moccasins that need mending are all brought forward and then every one is busy mending holes & tears in knees and feet. The snow shoes are all turned up at the toes, somewhat after this fashion.

Some of them have a string from the point of the shoe to the point of one toes. Edward has the string as his point is called na-na-da-doek, mine has a rounded point without a string and is called shim-nale. The dots all along the side near the fine lacing are made of little tufts of red or coloured wool which is not only useful in keeping the lacing fast but is also ornamental. Edward's shoes are about the usual man's size about 3 ft. 6 in long and 13 inches wide. Mine are about 2 ft 6 in long and 10 inches wide & the fine lacing is made of sinew and the thick part is narrow strips of skin.

SATURDAY 24 APRIL

We were all so disheartened that we did not care to start early for we thought we should have had a hard and weary day's work. We left our camp about 9 o'clock on snow shoes. Oh the snow was bad and we toiled on but soon we got into the trail and oh it was so much easier and we felt so thankful. In about an hour and a half we reached the top of the mountain after passing the top of the mountain we soon came to a lake such a pretty place and all frozen over. It looked such a famous place for skating though the ice then was not smooth enough. In the morning we crossed 4 lakes all very much the same. The scenery was very lovely. One had a small island in the middle & looked such a pretty place to live in but rather unget-at-able. In the afternoon the way got grander and grander. All our walk lay then between moun-tains, the mountains were so close together and we wound about round and round the foot of the mountains facing in turn nearly every point of the compass. The snow was very deep, some we measured 4 some 6 some 8 feet. The men have been complaining that their provisions will not hold out, they have finished their last salmon. We have finished our beef and small fish & have now for meat only bacon and an occasional grouse. They do not seem to understand the wisdom of saving, they eat as much if not more than they did when they had plenty, for they still have corn meal and oat meal. They know perfectly well that we have enough and if they finish theirs they will not go without. E asked one of them why they did not try to save if they knew that their provisions were short and the answer was that if he was to die tomorrow he should have plenty to eat today. They have been talking of dividing their packs on Monday and letting Liggy You-en (our best packer) go on with a small pack quickly and bring back some food for them. E and I have made up our minds that if we have to give them all this food we will not let Liggy You-en go. He knows the trail best.

SUNDAY APRIL 25

We got up very late for there was no work to be done and prayers about 12. Had mid day meal about 2, we went for a walk at 3:30 but it was so steep in all directions we soon came home again. There is one great drawback to camping out in this weather, when one gets into camp and gets dry it feels as if one were in heaven and to move off the mats & branches put down to be walked on one sinks so deep in the snow that one gets wet directly. Sometimes when the men leave the camp for water it is not unusual to see them sink knee deep or deeper for to put on one's snow shoes is a nuisance for snow shoes cannot be worn with boots. It was a glorious day and our camping place was very pretty among large pines. We measured the snow in different places and where it had drifted over & near logs we thought it was 10 feet. The average seemed 2 1/2.

MONDAY 26 APRIL

We left camp at 7. We were up at 4:30. The morning was bright, clear & cold & the snow dry & crisp. We started in moccasins but in about an hour put on our snow shoes. Shortly after we had put them on Liggy You-en, E and I were ahead when E saw a grouse and called

Pack horses nearing the Groundhog Summit, 5,700 foot elevation, on the Grease Trail. This photo depicts a barren, snow-covered landscape such as Kate describes in her journal. PHOTOGRAPHER: UNKNOWN. B.C. ARCHIVES E-08352.

Liggy You-en back for the gun. Liggy You-en left his pack at the foot of a tree and ran back and I went on slowly alone. The others were quite out of sight when to my great surprise I heard a dog bark quite close to me. I went on & in a moment met a man and 2 dogs. I was surprised to see him out not nearly so surprised as he seemed to see me. He stood and stared to see a white woman wandering apparently alone at that time in the morning in the forest primeval. I walked over to him & put out my hand and said "Good Morning," he did the same to me but there our conversation ended and we stood and looked at each other for neither of us could say any more. Soon E & L came up & L found out that he had come from the Kishpiyouks [Kispiox] village. He and his wife & child were camped some miles further on and he was then on his way up to the lake which we had just crossed to set his cage or trap for trout. The snow was splendid, it was the best snow shoeing we had had and we nearly flew, it was jolly fun. On, on we went and before lunch we made about 14 miles. We stopped in an old house for lunch & feasted on grouse which Liggy You-en & Sansanah had shot by the way. After lunch I went down & took a sketch of the bridge across the Kish pi youks river, a bridge which again we had crossed before we came to it. (For we crossed on the ice some hours before we reached the bridge). I found my (smoked) spectacles very useful for the glare was intense, in fact, I sketched with them on. When lunch was over the man we had met in the morning returned and the men went over to his camp and bought dried salmon and fresh bear which he had shot a few days before. We then went on as soon as we could for we knew with the afternoon sun the trail gets so bad. We went on for about a mile the snow was dreadfully bad, so bad that we took nearly 2 hours making that mile. The road lay over a wide country of bare hills. We at last came to a stand still, or rather a sit still for we sat down on a patch cleared from snow on the top of a hill where we had a consultation as to what was to be done for to go on was then a waste of time and we were all tired out. So though it was not quite 4 o'clock we said we would camp there and then and get up very early and set out by daylight in the morning. Liggy You-en took the gun to see if he could get grouse or rabbits. He got two grouse. E put up the tent but the ground was all rock & he could not put the pegs in & the wind was blowing so hard that it had to be put up strong so he got 2 trees & put them on each side of the tent on the ground & had to tie the loops of the tent to the trees. Sansanah & Dades got fire wood & branches for beds and I made bread. We had to go to bed very early. We told the boys that who ever was awake early must call & shout and get everyone else up. We said half past 2 would be early enough.

TUESDAY 27 APRIL

We were waked early in the morning by Dades. He got up & lit the fire, shouted to wake us—it was half past one—and we got up. I was afraid if we did not, he would turn into his blankets again, it was very cold. The wind had gone down a good deal but it was so frosty & cold. E got breakfast ready while I huddled my things on. Dades was employed thawing snow out in the tea pot for breakfast, for the little stream that we used the evening before was frozen, and had breakfast almost in the dark, though E lit one of his candles. The fire gave very little light & though the moon was up it gave very little light either. We left camp at 3:30 & it was hardly light. After going for a couple of hundred yards E stopped to fix my moccasins & we looked up and saw in a tree close to us 6 grouse. E ran back and Sansanah came up with the gun and shot one. The others flew away.

The snow was so slippery and glassy for it had thawed the day before & frozen again in the night. In some places it was very steep & sometimes they coasted down in their snow shoes. On one hill side all fell but no one was hurt. I had one fall which might have been a serious one. I fell forward & struck my head on the ice and knocked the skin off my nose between my eyes. It was wonderful I was not hurt. Liggy You-en had a bad fall too, he was coasting down a very steep place when at the very top he tripped in some way (the way they go is they lay one snow shoe on the other with the points at the back together & the toes a little way apart, then they sit on them & off they go) and instead of coming down sliding he rolled over and over pack and all until he reached the bottom. He scratched the knuckles of one hand but was not more hurt. Then for a long way we went without our snow shoes. One's feet feel so "handy" (if that is not an inappropriate word to use) after having worn snow shoes they seem to take up so little room. We went about 17 miles before ten o'clock & then stopped for a meal, what, breakfast or lunch, I am not sure. We were very tired, the boys had shot 3 grouse and 1 rabbit so we had plenty of meat. We rested until nearly 12 o'clock, then on we went again for about a mile the snow by this time was soft so we thought we had done a good days work and we camped for the night. The fire was lit & the tent up & branches cut about 3 o'clock & we all lay down & slept. I had the tent the others slept all round here & there. Sansanah took the gun but got nothing. About 5 o'clock E prepared a meal and about 6 he told me that supper was ready. We all gradually waked up & had a meal. After supper was over we had "ish" again and I liked it much better than at first. Then after resting a little while E put up a small piece of paper on a black stump for them all to try and shoot at. The prize if any one hit it was a piece of chocolate or as we call it now "Ligit-tim-nash me-an-e."

"Meane" is tobacco & I told them [it] was my tobacco.[42] No one hit it
& so the prize was not given. We all turned into bed early for we were
tired out as we had been up so early & walked so far.

WEDNESDAY 28 APRIL

We got up early so as to have a good start as the snow is good early.
Sansanah called us at 3:30 & we got up and got off at 5. The country
just here is very open & so the snow did not last good for long. Sansanah took the gun but saw no grouse. We saw three but as we were
going a short cut with Liggy You-en we could do nothing. L took my
stick & threw it at one & hit it but it flew away. We crossed several
streams and about 9 o'clock reached a large lake on which we hoped to
cross as it would save a long tramp around. The ice looked good except at the edge so E cut down some alders and threw them on the ice
for us to walk on. We got along beautifully for a time but as we got
towards the middle the ice began to be very bad. We could feel it give
at every step. The ice is in layers, the top layer about 5 inches thick,
then the stronger ice is below. The top layer crushed in at nearly every
step, so we made for a point on the shore about half way down the
lake. As we neared the shore the ice got worse and worse until in the
end E & L went through deeper & deeper at every step and near shore
they went in knee deep. I looked for a dry place to stand in while E
went ashore & put down his pack & then came back & carried me,
greatly to the amusement of Liggy You-en. We got on the top of a
bleak hill just at lunch time. It was the place where we met the summer
trail so we waited for Sansanah, we were very hungry, for it was about
11 o'clock. We lit a fire & cooked lunch. We boiled our peaches in the
tea pot for Sansanah had the pot and frying pan & then made coffee &
had a very good meal. The coffee is most delicious. When Sansanah
came up (in about an hour) and when the others had had their meal
we all felt tired and lazy. We had made about 15 miles so we said we
would stop then & there. It was a miserable place to camp, there were
no good branches for beds for there were only 2 small pines near &
they were very coarse. There was no wood near. They had to haul it a
long way, but there was water & it was clear from snow, so E said if
they could get enough branches to make a bed we would stop. They
agreed & off they went. They got all the branches that were to be had
& we stopped. It was so steep that they put an upright peg at the lower

side of the fire to prevent it rolling down hill & in the afternoon when Sansanah went to sleep he put a large piece of wood across to put his feet against to keep himself up. We put our tent cross wise on a ridge. E was on the lower side & had to put all the bundles & bags, boots etc that we could spare on the down side to keep himself up. We went to bed early for they said we were only 15 miles from Ankihtlast and we intended to be up very early & to make if possible, the other 15 miles before 10 o'clock.

THURSDAY 29 APRIL

I gave my watch to Sansanah the night before so that he might wake us early. None of them knew much about a watch but I thought the grandeur of the thing would help to wake Sansanah. He called us exactly at 2. Up we all got and breakfasted and packed up and left our last camping ground at 4 o'clock the sky was dark with clouds & the moon was up but it had not frozen much in the night & at first the snow was rather bad as we went on the snow improved. It was very hard frozen. E said he thought that it was freezing then. Some one had gone over the trail the day before when the snow was soft & had left deep tracks and now that the way has frozen the walking was very hard for a time. The sun when it was up for some little time became very hot but there was a cool breeze. We soon took off our snow shoes when ever the snow was gone for it was "shint" as they said, that means summer. We put them on and took them off about a dozen times. At about 9 o'clock we stopped to have something to eat. All our bacon was gone. E had no more powder so we could get no grouse, so we had coffee and bread & butter (our last butter) we gave the men oatmeal for they had no food (we gave them nearly all their food for the last few days) and after a little rest off we went again. They said we had gone about 11 or 12 miles I said 13, so they all said this was our last meal as we would reach Ankihtlast early in the afternoon. Some said 3 others said 4, others 5. We took off our snow shoes for good for we saw "shint" a long way ahead and on we toiled, sometimes on the trail, sometimes no trail to be seen. Through streams, through snow, over logs, through thick bushes, pushing & toiling along. In some places the trail was clear & easy but these were not many. The sun was very hot and as I had lost my sunbonnet the morning before I missed it sorely. (I used to have it on the outside of E's pack until about 8 or 9 or 10 in the morning til the sun was hot then put my hat in instead & wear my bonnet but when it was time to put it on, it was gone). We toiled on till 2 in the afternoon taking very little rest. E said then that we must rest for an hour that we were about 8 miles from Ankihtlast. The way seemed growing longer & longer and not shorter. We stopped for an hour in a shady place but I could not stay awake. E told me not to go to sleep as I would only feel more tired after. But as we sat there I dropped off. At 3 we went on again & in a few minutes came to a place where the trail was a running stream. There was no way to get round it for it was a large swamp. We walked through, it was only to our ankles. Oh I was worn out & the water felt so miserably cold. Sometimes we walked through snow through which we sank about 10 inches with water underneath. Oh we were wretched. We thought it all very, very bad but soon it got worse, infinitely worse for we came to water that was so deep it was up to the men's knees. E said that he would not let me walk through as I was wet enough & miserable enough already & as he was much wetter he would carry me. It was a long way & there was no way to get around. He carried me twice but the third time I begged & begged to be let walk for I knew it would be ever so much worse if in carrying me he should trip. He would not listen but took me up. And when we got to the deepest part he tripped and over he rolled on his back, his pack kept him from going underneath, but he was all under water but one shoulder & part of one side & head. He lifted me up. How I don't know, but he held me up at arms length above him & with one jump & plunge I got into shallow water only up to my ankles. We soon came to a part that was worse. It was over the men's knees. I insisted I would not be carried as I knew how wet I was likely to get if we fell. The end of my jacket was wet and ends of my petticoats from our little fall before. In we plunged and though I did not go over my knees in water for I jumped from place to place where it looked shallowest, E & the other men went above their knees. This walking lasted on and off for about quarter of a mile a little over E says. Now & then we would get on a tuft of grass or roots of trees or willow bushes in the water but the rest of the time we were wading & plunging through the water. E wanted to stop & camp for he said Ankihtlast was certainly 6 miles off but we were so wet that I thought we ought to press on. The boy with the blankets had gone on & I thought it was too bad to think of his having to come back. At last E cried out that dry land appeared. Oh we were thankful. We got along much better but the way was weary. The idea of saying in the morning that we had to go 15 miles, it felt far more like 150. The trail got better & clearer as we went on & we had good walking nearly all the rest of the way. We did not reach Ankihtlast till 7 o'clock worn out, so tired I could hardly walk. Little Robert saw us first & ran down to meet us. Then the whole family came. Robert says we went not less than 20 miles & that mostly over a fearful way. No trail in some places. At last our walk was over, our journey completed. We found Alice & all with colds. Baby is still baby she has not been baptized yet & they have not settled on a name yet. She is to be baptized soon. She is to be taken to the Forks to be baptized for I believe Mrs Hankin[43] is to be one God-mother.

It appears that Kate's intention was to stay at Ankihtlast for just a few months, but apparently she delayed departure and was caught in the

"Ankihtlast Mission," 1880.
Pencil sketch by Helen Kate Woods. B.C. ARCHIVES PDP01687.

weather.[44] As it turned out, Robert Sr. was to leave for England on urgent church business and so Kate stayed on to help Alice during his absence. Robert returned to the Skeena in February 1881.[45]

Little is known of Kate's activities while at Ankihtlast. If she continued writing a journal, it has not survived. In the B.C. Archives are two scrapbooks which contain Kate's pasted-in sketches. The sketches include several views of the mission, the Kispiox River and the wooden bridge at Hagwilget on the Bulkley River, and various other views in the Kispiox, Bulkley and Skeena areas. Some of these sketches are dated, so we have a sense of her movements. She spent time in Hazelton with the Hankin family, who lived at Roseberry Farm, and with the Bishop and Mrs. Ridley.[46] Her sketches sometimes contain brief notations about the significance of the scene or the point of view. Several of the sketches are included here.

"Ankihtlast," ca. 1880.
Pencil sketch by Helen Kate Woods.
B.C. ARCHIVES PDP01686.

"Canõn on the Kishpiyouks River," March 2, 1881.
Pencil sketch by Helen Kate Woods.

"Skeena Forks at Hazelton," November 15, 1880.
Pencil sketch by Helen Kate Woods. B.C. ARCHIVES PDP01680.

"Indian Bridge over Aquilket [Hagwilget] River, over 100 feet long & 3 ft broad,"
November 13, 1880. Pencil sketch by Helen Kate Woods. B.C. ARCHIVES PDP01682.

"Aquilket River above bridge," November 13, 1880.
Pencil sketch by Helen Kate Woods. B.C. ARCHIVES PDP01681.

"Roseberry Farm," 1880. Home of Thomas and Margaret Hankin.
Pencil sketch by Helen Kate Woods. B.C. ARCHIVES PDP01683.

"Vale of Ankihtlast, from Mission House. View from My Window," February 1, 1881.
Pencil sketch by Helen Kate Woods. B.C. ARCHIVES PDP01688.

"Kitselass Canon," May 2, 1881.
Pencil sketch by Helen Kate Woods.
B.C. ARCHIVES PDP01677.

An important document is the *Hazelton Queek*, "an editorial oddity that pioneered newspaper publication in Central British Columbia."[47] This was a handwritten single-sheet weekly "publication" run off on a gelatin duplicator. The first issue is dated 18 December 1880 and the last March 1881. Some 13 issues are extant. Apparently the *Queek* grew out of a need for communication amongst the white communities in this part of the Skeena. Kate later recalled:

Wishing to do all possible to help the whites, Mrs. Ridley started what she called pleasant evenings on every Tuesday and her house was open house especially [to] the men who came out from Omenica [and were wintering in Hazelton]. An evening of readings, music and general social intercourse. This social evening developed into a desire for a weekly paper. Both the Bishop and Mrs. R. were talented & had taken many sketches locally. Mrs. R. and I going out together, sketching up the Haguilket Valley. There was no news coming in for the winter

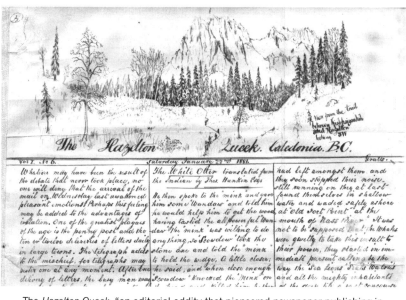

The *Hazelton Queek*, "an editorial oddity that pioneered newspaper publishing in central British Columbia." It was hand-printed and run off on a gelatin press. Thirteen issues were created between late 1880 and early 1881. Kate Woods contributed to the illustrations, as did Bishop Ridley.

months from the outside world we were absolutely cut off till spring would come. So everyone was expected to help in gathering items of interest, a riddle, a story, anything. My brother sent weather readings from our mission station. I contributed a few sketches for our paper was an illustrated one, and we looked forward to receiving it on Saturday. The B[isho]p wrote out and transferred it on a gelatine press sufficient numbers for the regular customers. About 10 or 12 I suppose. The Hankins, ourselves, & the miners, the B[isho]p.[48]

After Kate's return to Victoria, she married John Alexander Andrew at St. John's Church on 12 September 1882. Andrew was "an Irishman by race but was born in the East Indies, where his father was an officer in the British service."[49] He arrived in Victoria during the Cariboo gold rush and for many years was in the employ of the Hudson's Bay Company. Nothing is known of their courtship, although as a long-time Victoria resident, Andrew must have known the Woods family. An oral reminiscence states that they knew each other as children,[50] yet Kate was 13 years younger than her husband. We do not know the motivation for her marriage, if not love. The mysterious circumstances of her decision to escape from Victoria in 1880 might be tied to Andrew, or perhaps another love affair. Kate was 28 at the time of her marriage. Of her three older sisters, only Alice had married; her two other sisters were single and would remain so. Perhaps the urgency of her years, or perhaps a wish for economic security, contributed to her decision to wed. Of motivation we can only speculate.

Kate bore five children between April 1884 and October 1891. The family lived at the Woods home, Garbally; Kate's father had died in 1876 and her mother in 1883. In the summer of 1891 tragedy struck when John Andrew died very suddenly of cholera. Kate was widowed at 38. Her husband left an estate totalling some $7,500, which should have been enough to sustain the family; however, very soon they were destitute.[51] Kate had to look for work. She began teaching art in the schools, as her sister Emily had for several years already. Soon Garbally was sold, and the family moved into rented quarters. Kate moved to Vancouver when her children reached adulthood. She died in 1937 at the age of 83.

John Alexander Andrew, the man Kate Woods would marry in 1882.
PHOTOGRAPHER: UNKNOWN. PRIVATE COLLECTION.

Kate and John Andrew and their first two children, Patrick John Alexander, born 1884, and Richard Woods, born 1885. Kate bore three more children: Amy Kathleen in 1887, Winnifred Anne in 1889, and Emmeline Mary in 1891 (three months after her husband's untimely death). PHOTOGRAPHER: UNKNOWN. PRIVATE COLLECTION.

Reading Kate's journal in its entirety provides an insight into her strength of character. Despite the physical challenges of the journey, she appeared to enjoy herself. Her journal records the exhaustion, the dangers and the frightening situations encountered, yet she also writes about the lighthearted moments, the wonders of nature and her growing respect for her Indigenous guides. This respect begins when she comments that she will call Sansanah by the name his peers use, rather than the English nickname "Gumboots" that she and Edward initially used to substitute for the more difficult pronunciation of his Nisg̱a'a name. On another occasion, Kate wrote: "at first I felt highly disgusted at every thing I saw...." But it is only a week or so later that she confesses: "I often find myself doing things most extraordinary things...things I would have been horrified at before." Kate began to be comfortable with the different ideas about cleanliness, eating styles, priorities and world views of her guides. Toward the end of the journey she even envies them their freedom from convention and routine, saying: "for they live in such a free and easy style, everyone doing what he or she thinks fit.... It must be so much easier just each one to suit themselves." Out on her own, away from immigrant standards of living, Kate gained a new awareness, respect and understanding of the Indigenous people she met.

Once at Ankihtlast, she was thrown into the routine of mission life. The Indigenous population at the mission is not known, but an estimate of that population for the upper Skeena/Kispiox area in 1881 is 211, and for that at Hazelton, 199.[52] The settlers at Hazelton and the Tomlinsons at Ankihtlast were very isolated from other newcomers, but like the Agassiz family, they banded together as best they could to support each other emotionally, assist in times of hardship and socially interact when distances and weather conditions made it possible.

NOTES

1 Richard Woods (1813–1876) was Registrar of the Supreme Court of Vancouver Island. In 1870 he also became Registrar for British Columbia. He was appointed Sheriff for Vancouver Island in 1873, and "registrar of marriages and collector of votes for Esquimalt district" in 1875. In 1876, after a short illness, he died at Garbally, the family home in Victoria. His wife, Anne Woods (1813–1883), was involved in various philanthropic endeavours including, from ca. 1863 to 1868, a women's committee canvassing for donations towards a female infirmary.

2 A transcript of these reminiscences was quoted in the *Colonist*, 3 April 1960.

3 Bishop George Hills (1816–1895) arrived in Victoria in January 1860. He was the first Bishop of Columbia. His diocese, which covered Vancouver Island and the mainland, was funded by Baroness Angela Burdett-Coutts. In 1879 the diocese was split in three. See Roberta L. Bagshaw, *No Better Land. The 1860 Diaries of the Anglican Colonial Bishop George Hills* (Victoria: Sono Nis Press, 1996).

4 Charles T. Woods (1825–1895) arrived in Victoria on 23 August 1860 and assumed charge of the Boys' Collegiate School. His wife Maria, née Kingsmill (1827–1895), followed him, arriving via the *Brother Jonathan* on 8 November 1860. She became superintendent of the Ladies College, also run by the Anglican church. See references in Hill's diary, 1860, quoted in Bagshaw. For information on his later life, see endnote references in chapter on Violet Emily Sillitoe.

5 A transcript of reminiscences was quoted in the *Colonist*, 3 April 1960.

6 Information contained in oral interview with Winnifred Kirkpatrick-Crockett, daughter of Kate Woods. B.C. Archives.

7 Garbally Road was not cut out until the occasion of Alice Woods' wedding in 1868. See Elizabeth Forbes, *Wild Roses at Their Feet* (Vancouver: Evergreen Press, 1971).

8 The school was named after Angela Burdett-Coutts, whose individual patronage established the Bishopric of British Columbia and the installation of George Hills as Bishop. In 1879 the diocese was divided into three and Hills retained Vancouver Island. See chapter on Violet Emily Sillitoe for further details. The building exists today as Mount St. Angela.

9 In 1869 Kate was listed as an Angela College "prizewinner" (*British Colonist*, June 1869). She was at the school the same year Florence Agassiz attended.

10 For further details on their marriage and courtship, see *Wild Roses at Their Feet*, and George Tomlinson, *Challenge the Wilderness* (Anchorage: Great Northwest Publishing and Distributing Co., 1991) as well as interviews recorded with Tomlinson family members, transcribed in Margaret Whitehead, *Now You Are My Brother: Missionaries in British Columbia* (Victoria: B.C. Archives, 1981).

11 Edward Cridge, diary, 1868, B.C. Archives.

12 Ibid.

13 See *Challenge the Wilderness* for an account of the trip.

14 "Ankihtlast" is Gitxsan for "where bark is stripped." See *Challenge the Wilderness*, p. 184.

15 Apparently Archdeacon Charles Woods visited Kincolith in October 1871, following the illness of Alice with typhoid fever and her subsequent miscarriage. Reference in E. Palmer Patterson II, *Mission on the Nass* (Waterloo: Eulachon Press, 1982). Pinpointing particular years to some events in the lives of Tomlinson family members has proven difficult.

16 *Challenge the Wilderness* is often confusing with regard to dates, which at times appear at odds with the official records. The most obvious case in point is that author's story of the arrival of Kate Woods at Ankihtlast.

17 A journal was kept by Alice Tomlinson of this journey. The journal dates from 17 April to 9 July 1879 and includes entries by her brother Edward and husband Robert. MSS 2725, B.C. Archives.

18 See *Challenge the Wilderness* for anecdotal remembrances. Edward married this young woman, Alice Emily Percival, on 28 March 1881 and brought her up to the Skeena, where it became clear very quickly that she was not suited to the lifestyle. They returned to Victoria and eventually moved to Salmon Arm. It is possible that Kate returned to Victoria with them.

19 Margaret Hankin at Skeena Forks.

20 There is no firm evidence suggesting the source of this emotional turmoil. Descendants have always believed it to be an unhappy love affair.

21 Apparently she was unable to get out before the 1880 fall weather descended. This is family lore, repeated in oral interviews. Winnifred Kirkpatrick Crockett (née Andrew), B.C. Archives.

22 Schutt was the successor to Tomlinson, appointed to Kincolith on Tomlinson's departure for Ankihtlast. The Schutts and their three daughters remained until 1881.

23 The identity of these guides has not yet been determined.

24 MSS 773, B.C. Archives.

25 It is probable that Edward also kept a journal, as Kate's entries are labelled as Appendices, but there is no evidence of its survival. The journal was edited and revised in later years by Kate's daughter. A comparison of this revised account with the original

journal shows not just a cleanup of grammar and sentence structure and abridging of details, but also the inclusion of new facts as well as some explanatory detail not present in the original. These details are of such a nature to also suggest the existence of Edward's own journal, which may have been used to amplify certain facts, or else the addition of commentary by Kate many years after the fact. Such additions, when they improve or provide additional facts, have been incorporated here within the body of footnotes. The journal itself is reproduced here in its entirety and has been formatted only for consistency, interpreting dashes and dots as periods or paragraph breaks. The original spelling of the Nass River as "Naas," as used in the nineteenth century, is retained. Similarly the word "Nishka" is retained, whereas today we would more usually write "Nisga'a." Kate's phonetic spelling of personal and place names and other Nisga'a words has also been retained, although the current usage for place names has occasionally been inserted in square brackets to avoid confusion.

26 Apparently this means "remembrances," according to revised version.

27 John Byron Nice (d. 1940).

28 In 1879, Captain Henry Croasdaile built a salmon cannery half a mile above Fort Point on the Nass River. See Gladys Young Blyth, *Salmon Canneries: British Columbia North Coast* (Lantzville: Oolichan Books, 1991). In 1881, the Canada census enumerated ten white and ten Chinese residents at the cannery.

29 A reference to her sister Elizabeth.

30 Arthur was apparently a lay preacher and teacher at the school at Kincolith. In February 1880, Schutt's report to the Church Mission Society states: "A native teacher was conducting one of the three Sunday services." Quoted on p. 76, E. Palmer Patterson II, *Mission on the Nass* (Waterloo: Eulachon Press, 1982). "An Indian Christian layman, 'Arthur,' resided there [at Aiyansh] as a regular missionary agent." p. 117.

31 Listed in 1881 Canada census by enumerator Robert Tomlinson as "Ligeyoein, aged 30, a hunter from Kispiox." This is a possible identification for this guide.

32 "Bob, a Prussian", is how he is described in the revised version. *Williams British Columbia Directory*, 1882, lists a "W.W. Wand, foreman of the cannery."

33 No information about Matheson has been located.

34 Possibly Catherine Ryan, a young widow with four children romantically linked with Schutt, although this was denied by both Ryan and Schutt. Peter Murray, *The Devil and Mr. Duncan* (Victoria: Sono Nis Press, 1985), pp. 222, 130.

35 The revised version reads: "and kept up a constant moaning cry 'i-you-wah i-you-wah' (Oh dear, oh dear) but according to Indian custom no one took any notice...."

36 Revised version gives this meaning.

37 Revised version adds the information "with a population of not more than 50."

38 The scene of an old camp used by miners making their way to the Omenica gold mines.

39 John Andrew might be J.A.

40 Revised version reads: "We bought from one of them some 'Mi' (cakes of dried berries which are eaten as we might eat figs. Pressed into cakes, or soaked in water till looks like stewed fruit and is thought a great delicacy) and 'ish' (also berries, dried in cakes, a small quantity of which with a little water is whipped till it froths like a 'souffle' and is really palatable)." Ish is probably soapallalie, a delicacy known throughout the northwest coast.

41 Revised version adds: "Liggy You-en who had already been on the trail 13 times went first."

42 Revised version adds: "Once seeing me chewing chocolate, I told them it was tobacco so they call it 'the lady's me-a-ne."

43 Thomas Hankin (ca. 1843–1885), a former employee of the Hudson's Bay Company, married Margaret McCauley in 1871. They operated a store, hotel and saloon at Hazelton where Hankin was also postmaster.

44 Oral tradition in the family provides this explanation. Winnifred Kirkpatrick-Crockett to Willard Ireland, Provincial Archivist, 20 January 1960. B.C. Archives.

45 See Murray, p. 144, for details of Tomlinson's situation at the time. *British Colonist*, 25 February 1881, announced his return.

46 See notices in the *Hazelton Queek*.

47 Vancouver *Daily Province*, 11 February 1950.

48 Undated memo by Kate accompanying issues of the *Hazelton Queek* deposited in the B.C. Archives.

49 "Mr. J.A. Andrew." *British Colonist*, 18 August 1891.

50 Winnifred Kirkpatrick-Crockett to Willard Ireland, Provincial Archivist, 20 January 1960. B.C. Archives.

51 The estate may have been embezzled. Personal conversation, 1997.

52 Figures based on census returns, as quoted in Cole Harris, *The Resettlement of British Columbia* (Vancouver: University of British Columbia Press, 1996).

VIOLET EMILY

sillitoe

1855–1934

Violet Sillitoe, ca. 1879. PHOTOGRAPHER: WALERY. CITY OF VANCOUVER ARCHIVES PORT. P745 (DETAIL).

In April 1880, while Kate Woods snowshoed through the Nass Valley, another young woman, VIOLET EMILY SILLITOE (née Pelly), began her own adventure. She and her husband, Acton Windeyer Sillitoe, newly ordained Anglican Bishop of New Westminster, travelled by steamer from England en route to British Columbia. Here Violet's new life would begin.

Transportation and communication between continents had improved greatly since the 1860s. No longer was it necessary to travel by ship around Cape Horn or by railroad across the Isthmus of Panama. Transcontinental railways eliminated the need for going around the United States; one could travel by rail from the Atlantic coast and arrive in San Francisco on the Pacific coast. Accommodation was not luxurious, but the frequency of the train schedules and the reduced time of travel more than made up for this. Years later, Violet recalled the actual process of getting to the province.

> The steamer on which we crossed the Atlantic, the Allan liner *Sarmation*, was the last word in luxury, as it was accounted in those days.... Luxury in those days meant a very different thing to what it does now. The best of staterooms was exceedingly small, with the regulation upper and lower berths, a narrow sofa opposite, and a small washstand facing the door. The cabin was lighted by an oil lamp enclosed in a ground-glass case, shared between two staterooms, and the light was very dim.
>
> Arrived in the Gulf of St. Lawrence we were caught in a huge ice-field and could neither go forward nor backward. It was a wonderful scene, ice in every direction as far as the eye could reach, and innumerable vessels of all sorts and sizes ere in the same uncomfortable plight as ourselves. Little fishing schooners and big ocean liners were

caught fast in the ice.... People were out on the ice amusing themselves. The ice was from 15 to 20 feet thick, but was getting rotten, so that we were able, after a delay of about twenty-four hours, to grind our way through, and we arrived in Quebec ahead of the other steamers.

The Union Pacific was the only transcontinental line, and though the trains were comfortable, there were no dining cars, and the meals provided at the stopping places during the latter part of the journey, to put it mildly, were not appetizing.

The voyage from San Francisco in the old *Idaho* was even worse, for the steamer was crowded to capacity with men engaged to work on the railway construction of the C.P.R.; which had just commenced on the Western Division, and at night all the floor space was covered with sleeping figures. These men were described elsewhere as the scum of the San Francisco market![1]

The Sillitoes arrived in Victoria and were met by Bishop George Hills and his wife, Maria Philadelphia,[2] who took them to their home, appropriately named Bishop's Close (situated on Burdett Street). Here they recuperated from the journey and prepared for the final leg, which would take them to their home base at New Westminster.

The kindness of our hosts and the cleanliness of the house and meals and the sweet scents of the flowers wafted in through the open windows, by very force of contrast, made it seem like a foretaste of Paradise. Mrs Hills was a wonderful gardener, and the Bishops' Close garden was one of the sights of Victoria, to which all visitors from other parts were taken as a matter of course.[3]

A few days later, on June 18, they left Victoria by steamer and arrived in New Westminster. Much to their disappointment, there was no house ready for them, but the Archdeacon and Mrs. Woods received them most hospitably at the Rectory.

We made our headquarters with them for nearly three weeks, the Bishop making trips of a day or two to Burrard Inlet, Ladner and the North Arm of the Fraser and other nearby places, I accompanying him.

Then a move was made to Yale, and we took up our abode for a while in the four-room Mission House, built many years before. It was here I began to wrestle with the difficulties of cooking and house-keeping.[4]

In 1880 British Columbia was a stunningly rich combination of endless forest, pockets of farmland, snow-capped mountains, rushing rivers and scattered settlements. It held two major urban centres, Victoria on Vancouver Island, with a population of about 6,000, and New Westminster on the mainland, boasting almost 2,000 people. Nanaimo was the next largest, with 1,700. The town of Vancouver was in its infancy. Canadian census figures place the total white immigrant population in the province at about 19,000, and the Indigenous population at about 29,000.[5] This latter was a mere fraction of its previous population, which has been estimated at about 300,000 in 1782.[6]

Until 1880, with the arrival of two more Bishops, the Church of England administered the province as a single diocese. The Church of England was only one of several Christian denominations with an active presence in the province. Not only did the clergy of these different denominations administer to the immigrant population, but they also focussed on converting the Indigenous people to Christianity; in fact, this was one of the fundamental objectives in establishing a formal religious presence. George Hills, ordained Bishop in 1859, was responsible for clergy and promotion of the gospel over a wide geographic area. As he noted in his 1860 diary, the act of physically moving from area to area within B.C. in the nineteenth century was not easy and was fraught with uncertainty. "Impassable indeed, much of it was, for horses, mules, & even for men, not without danger."[7]

The diocese was split in three in 1879, and the following year both Sillitoe and his counterpart, Bishop Ridley, came to the province. George Hills assumed responsibility for the Diocese of Vancouver Island, William Ridley[8] for the Diocese of New Caledonia (northern B.C.), and Acton Sillitoe for the Diocese of New Westminster. Sillitoe had a large responsibility. His diocese covered the area of the province from the Pacific coast to the Rockies and as far north as Quesnel and Barkerville.[9]

The Cariboo Wagon Road, stretching from Yale northward, was the only established transportation route. Rough and difficult trails suitable for horseback or foot travel were the alternatives in the rest of the province. The transcontinental Canadian Pacific Railway was several years from completion; crews had only commenced blasting in the Fraser Canyon in May 1880.

Both Sillitoe and Ridley were consecrated as bishops in England in 1879. Before they left England for their new postings, they each spent considerable time travelling and lecturing at parishes throughout England. They needed to promote interest in and draw financial support for their dioceses, which would be funded solely by benefactors and parish commitments. Their positions, "livings" and expenses associated with establishing and building churches and congregations were all financed by donations solicited in England by sponsoring bodies, in particular the Society for the Propagation of the Gospel, and several wealthy patrons. The most renowned patron was Baroness Angela Burdett-Coutts, whose

View from the Bishop's House at New Westminster, 1880s. B.C. ARCHIVES PDP01769.

New Westminster, B.C., 1884. Reproduced in *The West Shore*. B.C. ARCHIVES B09389.

philanthropy initially established the Anglican presence on the West Coast.[10] The bishops reported back regularly to "home committees", describing their activities and successes in promotion of the Anglican gospel.

New Westminster was to be the home base for Sillitoe, where he would receive his clergymen and return from excursions to the different areas of his diocese. His job was to hold together and increase the network of parishes and missions in the diocese. Sillitoe assumed supervision of clergy at parishes in Hope, Yale, Lytton, Quesnel, Barkerville and Kamloops. In time, other communities were added. In addition, a number of "Indian Missions" ministered to the Indigenous population.

Sillitoe's travels were important in maintaining the Anglican presence in the tiny, tucked-away pockets of settlement scattered across many miles. It was important for the clergy and parishioners that he make regular visits—they were both morale boosters and special events. Sillitoe and Violet travelled for most months of each year, visiting isolated families and communities and providing advice, comfort, friendship and religious inspiration to a dispersed population.

In 1880, for the months while the old archdeaconry at Sapperton, just outside New Westminster, was renovated, Violet and her husband travelled to acquaint themselves with the diocese and to meet the clergy. "For the first six months after we arrived in British Columbia we were homeless wanderers on the face of the earth, but this mattered the less, as from the very first the Bishop began travelling about, visiting the farming settlements, gathering the settlers together to see what support could be given for church work, and finding the best centres for churches; and wherever he went I went, too."[11] After several months in the interior, at Yale, at Hope and in the Okanagan, they arrived back in New Westminster on 26 October, much disappointed to find that work had progressed so slowly that S[aint] Mary's Mount (as the house was known) was not ready for them. As Violet later recalled:

> This time the Rev. C. Baskett[12] came to our rescue and offered us a room in his house, a very ramshackle building roughly built of material from some abandoned sappers' houses, for Sapperton was where

the Royal Engineers were located when they were laying out the city of New Westminster....

Our quarters (or perhaps I should say "quarter," as we had only one room) in Mr. Baskett's house were far from luxurious, although in a missionary magazine Mr. Baskett had been described as one of the city clergy "languishing in the lap of luxury" so different from the up-country missionaries, whose many hardships were feelingly described. In point of fact nothing could have been more misleading. Mr. Baskett led a most self-denying life, and in his home few luxuries found place. Even his bed was only a built-in bunk in a tiny place off the kitchen, and the house was so badly constructed that the four winds of heaven blew at their sweet will through it. The room given to us was the dining-room and in a small alcove was the bed. It measured 2 ft. 6 ins. in width, and, having to accommodate two people, was widened by a wooden bench out of the church, on which for mattress was placed the original red cushion that adorned the gubernatorial pew in S. Mary's Church and which was much worn by long usage. It was better, however, than the mattress proper, which was of flock, which had gathered into hard lumps like raw potatoes, and the solitary pillow was filled with the same material. However, extreme fatigue made sleep possible, or if not, there was the pleasure of contemplating the stars through the holes in the roof, or for change we could look down through the cracks and knotholes in the floor to see how three of the would-be clergy, who had arrived from England, were getting on, and who were housed in a kind of basement, possibly even more airy than the house. Mr. Sheldon, one of them, not having a sufficient supply of blankets, we noticed was sleeping under a violet funeral pall which he had annexed from the church.

Our stove was a very small sheet-iron one with a drum in the stovepipe for oven, and in which on the first day I baked a beefsteak pie. To my immense astonishment it turned out a success; I think a special providence watches over the efforts of the very ignorant, but how inhospitable I felt when I had cooked a joint or pie which I hoped might last at least for two meals and it was picked to the bone or the last scrap at the first one!

Fortunately for us the Bishop could turn his hand to anything, but this quality was by no means shared by the embryo clergy. One day the menu for dinner consisted of herrings. Now I could clean herrings when necessity called for it, but I could not eat them afterwards, and the Bishop was very quick to notice any loss of appetite on my part. I asked all three of the young men if they would undertake this job for me, and all with one accord made some excuse or other, so I was just settling down to my work when the Bishop came along, sized up the situation, and took over the job himself. It was just the same with the wood chopping; if Mr. Baskett was not on hand to help, the Bishop did it. One good, kind engineer's wife saved me a lot of work by baking the bread for us.

As it was I became ill with the strain, and in consequence we moved into our house when it was still far from complete, and shared it with the workmen. The move was made on the day before Advent Sunday, 1880, when we at long last acquired a home of our own, and never before or afterwards did anything seem such an acme of luxury, and though our friends prophesied all sorts of ills from damp walls, etc., nothing happened.[13]

Violet Sillitoe, as the wife of the Bishop, carried a daunting responsibility for a young woman of 24. She was expected to be a model for other women, a helpmate to her husband and a constant worker for the Anglican church. She may have envisioned her lot while in England, but the reality of arrival in a rough and new post-colonial society took some adjustment. She had to become aware of the internal politics within the social strata of the immigrant population. In addition, she was inexperienced in interactions with the Indigenous people, whose cultures differed so greatly from hers. Violet and her husband tried to overcome their unfamiliarity by making great efforts to meet them one-on-one in order to personalize their interactions and promote understanding. Sillitoe also strove to recognize the growing Chinese population by providing schools and churches for them. The growing numbers of Chinese people, drawn to British Columbia by the gold rushes and, later, by railway construction jobs, created an uncomfortable racial division within immigrant society. It was certainly a challenge for the Bishop, but more so for his wife. Sillitoe had a network of clergy to advise him and administer, while Violet was really on her own without the equivalent female support locally. Maria Hills lived in Victoria, and Mrs. Woods, wife of the archdeacon, may have given advice, but as the Sillitoes travelled fairly continually through the diocese, Violet had to find the answers herself.

Violet's adventures in the new land encompassed the experiences of her rough and ready travels and her domestic life. It was all new, all a novelty, and all strenuous. She was a great letter writer and kept her family aware of her doings through long missives, often written under trying conditions whilst in camp or on the road. In these letters she recorded her activities and adventures. Many of the letters to her mother were returned to Violet after her mother's death, and they formed the basis for her reminiscences. These small works, titled *Early Days in British Columbia* and *Pioneer Days in British Columbia*, were privately published in 1922 and 1923. The former was written, as Violet herself relates, "for the benefit of those who come after, [to tell] what I know about the beginnings of Church history in British Columbia."[14] The latter "are mostly of a personal nature. They have been jotted down at the request of relations and friends, partly from memory and partly from letters written at the time...[They] deal more with the little daily happenings and journeyings in the semi-pioneer days."[15]

Although the letters themselves appear not to have survived through time, they were undoubtedly accessible in 1899 to H.H. Gowan, who wrote an important biography of Bishop Sillitoe.[16] Gowan used Violet's letters and the accounts she wrote for various missionary publications[17] to add personal details and bring the story of Sillitoe to life. Because Gowan quoted many letters at great length, Violet's words come back to us through the years and are as fresh and vibrant as the days she wrote them. Her words paint wonderful pictures of remote locations and rough conditions of life. They record events soon after their occurrence and thus differ in style (and sometimes substance) from the reminiscences composed and edited from the perspective of many years. I have relied on both the letters, as quoted in Gowan's *Memoir*, and the reminiscences to bring together the selection of Violet's stories in this chapter. They describe travels in the Cariboo, Okanagan, Kootenays and the Fraser Valley. The trips cover the period from 1880 to 1892 and document a time before the completion of the Canadian Pacific Railway, when travel was possible only by buckboard over rough dirt road or on horseback along trails.

But to return to domestic doings, the following extracts provide details of Violet's new life and responsibilities.

Soon after S. Mary's Mount was completed and the workmen had left, the Bishop was called over to Granville on some business and was obliged to stay overnight, and for some reason or other I did not accompany him. By this time we had a Chinaman, and as Sapperton is some distance from New Westminster, he slept in the house. We also had two dogs, a collie and a black retriever, the latter a dog of great character, by no means good tempered, but very much attached to us. At about two in the morning on the night of the Bishop's absence, I was awakened from my first sleep by the dogs barking most furiously, and slipping on my dressing gown I ran downstairs, calling to the Chinaman as I passed. The dogs were throwing themselves against the front door, and when I opened it they tore off in the direction of the gate. After some time and after hunting round the outside of the house, for I thought it might be a telegram from or about the Bishop, I returned and called the dogs in.

Our dogs, although allowed in the house, were never permitted to come upstairs. When I was returning to bed the black retriever started to follow me, and when he did not obey my first order to go down, I spoke to him sharply, and for the only time in his life he growled at me. That night he slept on the bare boards outside my door, and was there when I came out in the morning and begged his pardon. He knew his duty was to look after me in his master's absence and intended to do it in spite of anything I said. The Chinaman never came out of his room at all, but told me that he had heard steps on the verandah, and in the morning there were footprints, showing that two men had been around and some tools left outside were missing. It was well for the burglars that I was not as quick as I might have been in waking and getting downstairs or they might have fared badly from the teeth of the dogs....[18]

St. Mary's Mount was built initially for use by Archdeacon Wright. The 1880 renovations enlarged it somewhat so that it was suitable for accommodating guests.

St. Mary's Mount, otherwise known as "Hotel Sillitoe."
Violet Sillitoe is shown with friends, on the verandah. PHOTOGRAPHER: UNKNOWN.
ARCHIVES OF THE ANGLICAN DIOCESE OF NEW WESTMINSTER.

Our house was often called Hotel Sillitoe, because all sorts and conditions of people, both invited and uninvited, came to stay with us. It was a holiday home for any of the workers in the Diocese, and when people were ill they came to be nursed and to recuperate; some of our guests were indeed angels that we entertained unawares, and owing to conditions and difficulties of travelling they would turn up quite unexpectedly. On one occasion at four o'clock one morning in summer time, the Bishop, hearing steps on the verandah, put his head out of the window and called, "Who is there?" A meek voice from below replied: "Me, my Lord." "Me" was the Rev. R. Small, later Archdeacon of Yale, and his colleague, the Rev. H. Edwardes, who had just arrived from Lytton.[19] I was getting up to make beds ready for them, when I was ordered to remain where I was. I had been ill and was only just recovering. For the remainder of the night the two men had to sleep between blankets, to the great distress of my housewifely soul.[20]

The Sillitoe home was also the logical place to accommodate visiting dignitaries, as the local hotels were somewhat lacking in refinement.

During our sojourn at S. Mary's Mount we had the honor of enter-taining three governors-general. Princess Louise accompanied her husband, the Marquis of Lorne; Lord Lansdowne was only accom-panied by his staff, while Lady Stanley of Preston came out with her husband. In each case our house, which was none too big, was taxed to the limit, and beyond.

The Marquis of Lorne was the first one to come, in the early autumn of 1882. His party consisted of H.R.H. the Princess Louise, with her two ladies-in-waiting, Miss McNeill and Miss Harvey; Col. De Winton, comptroller of the household; and two valets. Other members of the party we found room for in the old Government House and in town.

We had only twenty-four hours notice of the honor in store for us, and, as usual, it found us with every room in the house occupied; in-deed I never remember the time when the house was not full. We had, therefore, not only to provide for the incoming guests, but to find quarters for the outgoing ones. Staying with us at the time were two of the Cowley Community, Fathers Hall and Shepherd, who had come out to spend the summer ministering to the men working on the Canadian Pacific Railway construction. Later Father Hall became (and still is) Bishop of Vermont, while Father Shepherd died in South Africa.

I was still very young at the time, and very shy, and stood in great awe of these two holy men, but when they asked if they could do any-thing to help, my need of assistance was so great that I promptly accepted, and giving them two big aprons, set them to work to clean the silver! Like everything else they undertook, the work was done to perfection! Miss Kendal,[21] who at that time was in charge of Columbia College, the Church school for girls, was also most kind in helping me.

S. Mary's Mount had three fair-sized bedrooms and two very small ones, and into these the party was packed, H.R.H. and the Governor-General having our bedroom and one of the small rooms as dressing-room, the two ladies-in-waiting sharing a room, and Colonel de Winton occupying the remaining large one. The Bishop and I and all our possessions were piled into the second small one, which was about six feet by ten or twelve, with no cupboard. I shudder when I think of the appearance of that room. The party arrived at about 1 o'clock and in great style, for there being no carriage on the mainland, other than the high, old-fashioned stages, a landau had been imported for the time being from Victoria.

A party of bluejackets formed the escort. As the luggage was to follow later, the Princess asked if she might borrow one or two articles from me, and happily amongst the wilderness piled up I was able to find what she needed. Amongst other things, put in at the last minute [to the room temporarily taken over by Violet and the Bishop], was our little dog, who was apt to bark at strangers.

When the Princess came downstairs she said to me: "I hope I have not done wrong, but when returning your belongings I let out your little dog!" Just imagine my feelings at H.R.H. having seen that awful room!

The Princess told me to be sure to make use of the valets—these two men having been accommodated with tents pitched in the field at the back.

If I had been awed at the thought of entertaining royalty, I was simply terrified at the valets, but again extreme need came to my aid. Our domestic staff consisted of one Chinaman, who had to look after the horses, milk the cow, attend to the vegetable garden, besides cooking, baking and washing for the family, and help, therefore, was urgently needed, so I had the head valet in, giving him directions as to the setting of and waiting at table, etc.

I explained that I made the coffee myself in the drawing-room of which he quite approved, saying that H.R.H. did the same at Government House, but when I further explained that after returning from viewing the torchlight procession and illuminations on the river, I wanted him to bring in the tea tray, which I would have all ready, there his approval ceased—"We don't have tea at Government House, madam!"

Feeling that I must assert myself, I said: "I think I would like you to bring it in," and he added rather apologetically: "You see, madam, our gentlemen don't drink enough to require it!" His enlightening of my unsophisticated mind on the reason of tea and coffee after dinner was so deliciously funny that I had to go into the drawing-room to repeat the conversation, which caused much amusement.

Princess Louise was an ideal guest, so simple and unassuming, as were the ladies-in-waiting. Miss Harvey was a first-rate musician. Miss McNeill afterwards married, as his second or third wife, the old Duke of Argyle, and so became step-mother-in-law to Princess Louise.

The Princess made several sketches from our field and these appeared later in the *London Graphic*. As it was still too early for fires, she went into the kitchen herself to dry her sketches, catching the Bishop at the back of the house in his shirt sleeves doing some necessary chores. Between tea and dinner we spent the time with music, the Princess and I singing duets, she taking the alto and I the soprano.

Next morning there was a great gathering of Indians to see the "Queen's Papoose" and also to make speeches to the Governor-General. Just before leaving, Colonel de Winton came in to tell the Princess what arrangements had been made, for she was to return to *H.M.S. Comus* that day en route for Victoria, and the whole party, ourselves included, were to go with her to Port Moody. The Marquis was to return with us, as he was going on up country next day. The arrangements were that the Governor-General, the Princess and the two ladies-in-waiting should drive in the landeau, the Bishop and I in the buckboard, and the rest in all sorts and conditions of buggies and stages.

"Oh, no," said the Princess, "that won't do. I am going to drive in the buckboard with the Bishop," and no amount of persuasion or expostulation would turn her from her purpose.

This was the first the Bishop had heard of the honor in store for him, and he hastily slipped out to the stable to have a look at the harness and see to the harnessing of the horse. The buckboard had seen service, hard service, and indeed very little of its original coating of paint remained, while the harness had been secondhand when we bought it and had since then grown perceptibly shabbier, and although not held together (as much B.C. harness was) by cord and telegraph wire, still it was only a few degrees better.

"Punch" my beautiful horse, given to me on my first birthday in British Columbia by the Bishop, had blue blood in him. He was bred for a racer but had ignominiously failed in his first race, and the Bishop, therefore, was able to acquire him for the price of an ordinary horse. But even "Punch" did not appear at his best. His coat was shaggy and none too well groomed; in fact, the whole turnout, to say the least, was appallingly shabby. It headed the procession, passing through the decorated grounds to the playing of the bands, the waving of flags and the cheering of the crowds.

Next came the landau with the Governor-General and myself, and the two ladies-in-waiting opposite. The honor thrust upon me was not at all appreciated, and I sighed for the buckboard and the company of my husband. We all lunched on the *Comus*, returning in the afternoon, and next day, after bidding adieu to the Marquis of Lorne, we returned to our ordinary daily round.[22]

Violet wrote about the royal visit many years later, and undoubtedly the passage of time toned down her recounting of her emotions at the time, which must have included sheer fear of failure, embarrassment of circumstances and awe of the situation that thrust her into such an intimate royal scenario. It was the first of several such hostings of important guests.

Violet's letters and reminiscences about her travels in the province provide important documentation for the historian. They not only provide intimate description of situations that are but footnotes in the grand recollections of provincial matters, but also give insight into the personal viewpoint of a woman of the times. In the letters especially, Violet recorded her inner turmoil, her worry, her joy and fascination. The following extracts document travel from 1880 through 1892.

In September, 1880, we made our first long journey into the interior, travelling over the Hope Mountain trail. This was our first experience in rough camping. This journey lasted six weeks, covering over 800 miles.

Between Osoyoos and Penticton we had an adventure which came near to ending our earthly career. We were asleep in our tent when we were awakened by a hurried call from the Indian. There was a curious, rumbling noise, which grew louder and louder, very much like an earthquake, and the ground seemed to shake beneath one's feet. The night was dark, and standing in the door of the tent it was impossible at first to see anything, but a cloud passing away from the face of the moon revealed a band of wild horses bearing down upon us at full gallop. As they came near and saw us they divided into two groups,

Columbia Street, New Westminster, September 1882. Decorated arch constructed in honour of the visit of Princess Louise and the Marquis of Lorne. The arch was intended to illustrate fishing, the city's most important industry. In keeping with this theme, it was built with salmon boxes and barrels filled with tins of salmon, placed in the shape of pyramids. The evergreen boughs adorning it were draped in fish nets. The inscription reads "Our Sea Farm. Natural Resources." This was one of several arches (different themes) erected in the city for the occasion. The Sillitoes and their honoured guests passed under the arch in the episode described by Violet.
PHOTOGRAPHER: UNKNOWN. B.C. ARCHIVES A-03406.

passing by on either side. Had the moon not come out they would have probably become entangled in our tent ropes, and we should not have lived to tell the tale.

Another, this time amusing, experience happened when we were in camp seventeen miles above Yale. Lying asleep in the tent early one morning, my head close up against the canvas, I was awakened by a noise that made me jump almost as high as the ridge pole. An ox from one of the travelling teams had wandered up to our tent and, putting his nose down to where my ear was, had suddenly given a loud sniff. I thought that surely it must be "the crack of doom." On this first inland journey we visited Osoyoos, Penticton, Okanagan Mission, Coldstream, Spallumcheen, Kamloops, Grand Prairie, Ashcroft, Lytton and Yale. At Coldstream we stayed with Mr. Forbes Vernon,[23] the younger of the two brothers from whom the town of Vernon takes its name.

Vernon from the east end of Barnard Avenue, ca. 1889.
PHOTOGRAPHER: UNKNOWN. B.C. ARCHIVES A-06940.

View of Yale from across the Fraser River, 1880.
PHOTOGRAPHER: UNKNOWN. B.C. ARCHIVES D-08808.

There was an unusually large congregation at the Sunday service, for the threshing machine was paying a visit to the ranch. A large airy barn was used as a church, boards being placed between boxes for seats. Everything went well until the sermon, when, just as the Bishop was giving out his text, a hen in the hay which was piled up on one side, having laid an egg, proceeded to announce the fact in ear-piercing tones. The Bishop waited until the hen had finished and again began his text, but this seemed to be the signal for the hen to repeat her announcement. In the meantime, Mr. Vernon, feeling terribly guilty, left the barn, and, climbing up on to the hay from outside, tried quietly to "shoo" the hen out, but instead of doing what she was wanted to, just as the Bishop for the third time began his text, down she flew into the midst of the congregation with shrieks which outdid all her former efforts, after which the service was concluded without further incident.[24]

One of the most distant outposts of the diocese was Barkerville, in the Cariboo District. Travel was by steamer to the head of navigation on the Fraser River, and then by buckboard along the Cariboo Wagon Road, which was built in 1862 by the Royal Engineers and considered a feat of engineering excellence. The road clung to the blasted-out cliff edge of the Fraser Canyon, perched on cantilevered cribbing, then followed the Fraser and Thompson Rivers to Quesnel and on to Barkerville. Travellers, dependent upon the strength of their horses, travelled distances of twenty miles or so each day, lodging at stopping houses named after the mileposts along the way.

Here is Violet's own account of her first journey along this route and of her adventures in the Cariboo mining district which had been the site some eighteen years earlier of the great Cariboo Gold Rush.

During the early days of the gold excitement a church had been built [at Barkerville] and a clergyman had been stationed there, a Mr. Reynard, but the hardships had been great and he only remained a short time, so that for many years past no clergyman had visited the upper country. The Bishop was anxious to pay a visit as soon as possible, but it was not until the late summer of 1881 that his other duties allowed of this. The river steamer carried us and our buckboard and horses as far as Yale. From there on we took the wagon-road. This road was an

"An Indian Gathering at Hope, B.C.," ca. 1884.
This large group includes several non-Indigenous people. Seated in the centre are Violet and Acton Sillitoe and the Bishop of Vancouver Island, George Hills. Other clergy stand behind them. Sisters from All Hallows School at Yale with their pupils are on the right.
PHOTOGRAPHER: UNKNOWN. B.C. ARCHIVES B-05522.

engineering feat, built right through the Fraser Canyon. It was 18 feet wide and has been described as "a road with a precipice on one side and an abyss on the other." Passing round the bluffs the road was built out on struts, overhanging the Fraser hundreds of feet below. One of the rules of the road was that the lighter conveyance should take the outside of the road, and ours was always the lighter conveyance. It was not a very pleasant thing to have to draw up at the extreme edge of the road while an ox team with six, eight or ten yoke of oxen lumbered past on the inside, with not an inch of road to spare. It took us about a fortnight to make the journey, which meant twelve travelling days and two rest days. The stage made the distance in much quicker time, but the stage travelled almost night and day, and had relays of fresh horses

Chapman's Bar Bluff, Fraser River, Cariboo Wagon Road (17 miles above Yale), 1867.
PHOTOGRAPHER: FREDERICK DALLY. B.C. ARCHIVES A-00354.

every fifteen or twenty miles. It was the Bishop's custom to call at every house on the road, irrespective of nationality or creed. Sometimes there were children to be baptized, couples to be married—even an occasional funeral. Arriving at our destination for the night, after the horses had been fed and cared for, and we had had our supper, the

Bishop would gather the people together for a service, and in the morning before starting off again, if there was just one communicant, there would be a celebration of Holy Communion. Everywhere we received the warmest of welcomes. But O! The loneliness of the lives of these settlers, and it came hardest of all on the women. The ranches were long distances apart, and, with exception of the few favoured ones, no female help could be afforded, nor indeed was it much easier where it could be paid for. Men were greatly in the majority, and a girl coming out from England soon found a home of her own. There were suitors a-plenty. I heard of one girl who, on the evening of her arrival, went to answer a knock at the door, finding a rather rough-looking settler on the doorstep, who evidently believed in coming quickly to

Cariboo Wagon Road at China Bar Bluff, Fraser River, 1882.
PHOTOGRAPHER: D.R. JUDKINS. B.C. ARCHIVES B-01443.

A view on the Cariboo Wagon Road at Yale, B.C., 1867.
PHOTOGRAPHER: FREDERICK DALLY. B.C. ARCHIVES H-02912.

the point, "If you please, Miss," he said, "I hear that you have just come out to this country; now I have a nice farm of 160 acres and a team of horses and some cows and pigs and poultry, and now I want a wife, and I thought, maybe as you would suit me." "Well, you won't suit me," she replied, slamming the door in his face. But the choice was large, and these girls were soon suited.[25]

The distances were great, and as much as it must have challenged Violet and her husband, there was an unvarying tedium to the days on the road.

Driving on day after day was monotonous work, at least to tell about, but sometimes the monotony would be varied by a deer, a bear or a panther crossing the road—sometimes even a cariboo; or we would look around and find that we were being stealthily followed by a coyote. At other times the monotony would be less pleasantly varied

"Three Mile Canon on the Fraser River showing primitive structures for drying salmon," 1867. PHOTOGRAPHER: FREDERICK DALLY. B.C. ARCHIVES A-04283.

when a windstorm during the night brought down one of the big trees for which British Columbia is famous, right across the road, and the underbrush was so thick on either side as to make driving round impossible. We would have to unharness the horses, lead them round and tie them up, and then would begin the work of getting the buckboard over. Here came in the advantage of having the lightest conveyance on the road, but getting it over was indeed a work of time, and the buckboard seemed to weigh tons and tons. It took every ounce of our strength, and left us exhausted and bruised. The worst things however, that we had to encounter were the forest fires. I cannot begin to describe how awful these were, the big trees crackling and burning on either side, falling every now and again with a crash, the air dense with smoke and the flames from the burning underbrush driven by the wind right across the road. My heart at such times seemed almost to stop beating from terror, and one's whole being concentrated into an act of prayer that God would bring us through this awful danger.[26]

Violet's understandable relief in attaining her destination safely and experiencing the luxury of staying put for a while was evident. "It would be difficult to realize the delight of reaching Barkerville, the journey's end, and feeling that one could rest without the thought of having to move on again next day. Nothing could have exceeded the warmth of the welcome given us by the miners, who had congregated from the outlying creeks. The little church was crowded to its utmost capacity, and the singing was of the heartiest."[27]

In August 1881, Violet wrote to her mother and described the week's events.

Early in the week we visited a mine about six miles distant. We had dinner in a miner's cabin, and though we were unexpected, the dinner that was very soon ready seemed almost the work of a conjuror. Chicken, beef, strawberries, and peaches were among the delicacies set before us (all canned, of course), and tea, without which no meal is complete in this country. After dinner we went down the 'Brothers' mine on Jack o' Clubs Creek. It is one hundred and eighty feet deep. We saw the process of getting out the earth and sending it to the surface to be washed. Some of it was 'panned' out, as it is termed, for me, and, much to the annoyance of the miners, who are most generous, the pan showed but few 'colours.' Still I carried away with me some specimens of gold dust. The 'Brothers' mine connects with the 'Sisters,' and we crawled through the low passage between the two, and came up to the surface by another shaft. Next day we went to see the wash-up of an hydraulic claim, and the same day went down another shaft, popularly known as 'slum tunnel' from the amount of slime and mud in it. I brought away two very pretty specimens of gold....

We left Richfield on Friday, and a large party assembled to see us off. Just before starting a note was brought me, which, upon opening, I found to be from the principal residents asking me to accept a beautiful gold nugget, the largest found in the 'Brothers' during our stay in Cariboo. This nugget I have now in the shape of a bracelet, with raised letters on it, and I shall always greatly value it in remembrance of our first visit. We stayed for a few hours in Stanley, and spent the night at Beaver Pass, a few miles further on. Next morning, before starting, the Bishop married a couple. Sunday we spent at Quesnelle Mouth, holding services in the schoolroom, and the congregation was so large that many had to leave, not finding room. Our journey down was not so enjoyable as that on our way up.

From Quesnelle Mouth to Clinton we had rain every day, and the roads were so fearfully muddy that we were obliged to walk the horses nearly all the way. The drivers of ox-teams told us they could only make four or five miles a day, having constantly to take the oxen out of the one waggon to hitch them on to the other team....[28]

At another time, Violet gives a dramatic account of camp life and ministering to the sick.

I am writing under difficulties, with a tiny gold pencil and my paper on my knee, under the shadow of the church. We are camped out near an Indian village on a dry, dusty, and exceedingly barren flat, under a burning sun, with not a tree nearer than on the steep mountain sides which surround us. I am hardly correct in calling this a barren flat, for on it thrives a vigorous growth of cactus, and with the utmost care one cannot go many yards without getting one's shoes full of the sharp prickles. One night in rolling over in bed I got my side full of them....
On Wednesday, July 29th, we drove down the waggon-road about fifteen miles, and after crossing the Thompson river in an exceedingly ramshackle canoe, and climbing the steep bank, we arrived at this our first camp, Pakyst.[29] Meshell[30] was there already, and had our tents pitched. As it was getting dusk, I lost no time in unpacking our blankets, and as on account of the great heat we needed none for covering, we had a less hard bed than would otherwise have been the case. After that we had our supper of bread and marmalade by the light of a candle, the candlestick consisting of three nails in the top of a piece of wood driven into the ground. After supper we retired to bed rather than to sleep, for a strong gale had sprung up, which threatened to carry our tent away, and in the course of the following day the threat was carried out, and I had to fly about in all directions gathering up my scattered belongings. We have stayed three whole days in this camp, and the programme has been much the same as at Ashcroft....
Pakyst was a comfortless, hot camp, and it was without any regret that we left it on Saturday, August 1st, walking three miles down the railway track to Spatsum station, while the tents and pack were sent

Lytton, ca. 1880.
PHOTOGRAPHER: UNKNOWN. B.C. ARCHIVES A-03553.

on horses over the trail. The west-bound train was due at Spatsum at 3am on Sunday, and the long, weary night did we spend sitting on the platform; and as if that were not enough, the train was an hour and a half late, so not till 4:30 did we get away. Spatsum is only a flag station, and about ten o'clock the man in charge brought us a lantern, telling us to wave it, and he then retired. It was 6:30 on Sunday morning before we reached Lytton.... It seems impossible that animals on four legs can walk as slowly as these Indian horses do. Arrived in camp, we found lots of Indians ready to help, and in a wonderfully short time the tents were pitched, a thick carpet of brush laid, and it was just getting dusk when we sat down to our supper, spread on the ground in front of our tent. After supper the Bishop arranged for the next day's proceedings with the Indians, while I made up the bed. Then we sat down over the camp fire, admiring the dim outline of the surrounding mountains, and the picturesque encampment about two hundred yards away in a grove of large pine trees, everything looking weird and ghostlike in the light of three camp fires. Then the stillness was broken by the sound of a bell summoning to prayer, and the whole camp gathered, and the low monotony of the voices sounded not unmusical, and wonderfully solemn and impressive, borne to us on the evening breeze…. At 10 pm we turn in, but alas! There are many disturbances. First of all, the camp fire spreads, a most dangerous proceeding during the dry, hot weather, and it has to be beaten out, and later on there is an ominous pitter-patter on the tent, increasing to a steady downpour, and the Bishop has to go outside and loosen the ropes. Then a careful look round is necessary, for if anything is touching the tent, in comes the wet; even the cabin bags had to be taken down.

It was still raining at six o'clock next morning, and the celebration had to be postponed, as our second tent, used as a church tent, is only big enough for the altar, and the congregation has to be in the open…. [W]e did not get away until 11:30, too late to allow of our reaching the next rendezvous, N'chakup Camp,[31] the same day. So we rode about twelve miles, passing on our way an Indian lying in his tent, ill from the bite of a rattlesnake. These reptiles are said to be very numerous in these parts, but from the fact that recovery from the bite is possible if the right remedy be used in time, I imagine they are not so deadly as in other countries. I am afraid I shall shock you if I describe the remedy; but remember it is a case of life or death. The bite is usually on the foot or leg, and a tight string is at once tied above the wound to prevent as far as possible the circulation of the poison in the blood. After that the patient is doused with raw spirit until the system becomes saturated. The poison causes intense pain, and it takes a long time for it to work its way out. As there is a strict law in force in British Columbia forbidding the sale of liquor to Indians except on an order from a clergyman, doctor, or J.P. it is no easy matter for them to obtain the required remedy in time. It is curious that the Indians, who are skilled in the use of herbs, should not yet have discovered an antidote. Our camping ground on the night of the 5th was a most unpromising one—near the bed of the creek, with nothing but rocks and sand, and it was too late to allow of much brush being collected, so our bed was none too soft, and the tent was badly pitched, so did not entirely keep out the rain which fell during the night. Towards six o'clock in the evening we reached N'chakup Camp, leaving the proper trail about half a mile back. Oh, if you could have seen that last half-mile I think your hair would have stood on end! First we skirted round a sandy, gravelly bluff—the trail was, I am sure, not more than six inches wide, and at every step the horses sent the stones and sand rolling down the

"Bishop Sillitoe's cottage," Lytton, ca. 1890s.
Quite possibly the home of Alphonse Hautier, with whom the Sillitoes stayed when
they were in Lytton. PHOTOGRAPHER: UNKNOWN. B.C. ARCHIVES B-05492.

precipice. Then we started zigzagging down the mountain side, and it was no easy matter to stick on the horses' backs. My contempt for Indian horses on a good road is unbounded, but in dangerous places and broken-away trails, my contempt changes to confidence and admiration....

At N'Chakup Camp we spent three whole days, and every moment of the Bishop's time, except what was grudgingly snatched for meals, was devoted to the Indians.... One afternoon we crossed the river in order that the Bishop might visit a sick child. The Fraser is extremely swift, and the boat had to be towed a long distance up the shore before the crossing was attempted. I have pretty strong nerves, and like being in a canoe; but this craft was an exceedingly cranky and leaky flat-bottomed boat, and was besides overloaded, and two or three times I thought we should have capsized. The sick child was lying under a kind of shelter made of rush mats. She was about seven years old, and did not look ill, but was lying quietly sleeping; and in this way her parents said she had been lying for the past three weeks, taking nothing but an occasional spoonful of cold water. We could give them but little advice, but sent them from the camp some condensed milk to mix with the water. Near the sick child sat an old Indian, stone blind, who was led forward to shake hands with us by his equally ancient spouse. A decrepit old pair they were, and not pleasant to look at.[32]

Winter travel was also a challenge. The following account describes a trip from Chilliwack to Yale and then back. The roads through the Fraser Valley paralleled the Fraser River, which in the winter of 1880–1881 was frozen over in many parts.

Our driver wished to start at seven the next morning (Friday), but we objected so strongly that he consented to make it eight o'clock if we would be punctual. It was he, however, who kept us waiting, and it was 8:30 before we made a start. Our conveyance was a very primitive one, a long shallow box on runners, a plank laid across as a seat, and, for my comfort, some hay behind to lean against. The day was very fine, not very cold, and the sun shining brightly. The road not being used except for a short time in winter, when the river is closed by ice, is not kept in repair, and a nice shaking we had, scrunching over stones, through the rocky beds of streams, and over other almost impossible places. There are dips in the road as deep as a ditch, and into these the sleigh goes, standing up on the front end, and then on the back. We had to keep in as best we could, since there was nothing to hold on by. At one place one runner was on the rock, and the other on the ground; the Bishop was on the lower side, and out he was thrown with one foot only left in the sleigh. I followed helplessly, and then came the hay. Happily, we were going slowly, and the driver noticed us, and pulled up. A yard further and we must have been deposited in the bed of a stream, which, although not deep, would have given us an unpleasant wetting.

Our driver told us there was one "bad" place, where the road goes round the face of "Murderer's Bar Bluff." A few nights before he was driving some of the mail passengers, and seeing they were quietly asleep, intended to drive round without waking them. One man, however, started up just as they were coming to the place, and seeing the character of the road, without a moment's hesitation rolled out at the back of the sleigh. It so happens that just at this part of the road there is no snow, but a smooth sheet of ice, with nothing to prevent the sleigh slipping off the road down into the river below. The sleigh got round safely, but the efforts of the passenger to get around on foot seemed hopeless. So slippery was the ice that he could not even stand, and at last had to take off his boots and follow barefooted till he succeeded in reaching the sleigh. Our autumn trip made us callous to such places, and we were driven safely round. At three o'clock we reached the Indian village of Oham'l,[33] and there stopped about an hour to rest the horses and get dinner, which was prepared for us by an Indian woman. There were not many people on the road, but we met one picturesque-looking Indian, with gun slung at his back, moccasins on his feet, snowshoes in his hand, and surrounded by five dogs. About 6:30 we reached Hope, the last part of our drive being in bright moonlight. We were tired, stiff, and very cold, but had thoroughly enjoyed our drive. Dock and Boundary, our two steeds, were as pleased as we were to have reached the end of their day's journey.

The Bishop had arranged that a team should meet us on the other side of the river on the following morning, Saturday, to take us on to Yale, and at half-past ten Captain Bristol, the mail-guard, came to say that a canoe was waiting to take us across. We started on foot over the hard snow, down the steep bank of the river, and then paddled across, landing on the ice on the other side about half a mile higher up. The ice was so slippery and the wind so strong, that had I been left to myself, I should have been reduced to take the same measures as the gentleman going round the Bluff. Happily, there was no necessity for this, as Captain Bristol had provided a small hand-sleigh, on which the Bishop and I seated ourselves, and we were drawn, or rather, the wind blew us, across the ice to the shore. The sleigh which awaited us was of the same description as that we had had the day before, only now it was nearly filled with goods, and we had nothing against which to rest our backs. Twice we had to get out when the sleigh went through streams, the bridges over which had been burned. It was thought more than probable that if we remained in the sleigh we should be overturned into the water. The snow on this side of the river was much deeper than on the other, and for about eight miles we could hardly advance beyond a walking pace. Nearer Yale there had been more traffic, and we progressed more rapidly. We found Mr. Whiteway and Mr. Blanchard[34] at the door of the Mission House to welcome us on our arrival, and very soon we felt ourselves quite at home again. Many Indians came to the Mission House in the course of the afternoon and evening to see the Bishop....

On Monday the Bishop was occupied the whole day arranging business matters and seeing people. On Tuesday morning we started homewards, the morning being fine and bright, though the East wind was very cold. During the night the thermometer had been as low as 10° Fahr. Thanks partly to the numerous wraps with which our sleigh was provided at Yale, we were warm enough, and the road being in better condition than it had been on Saturday, we managed our fifteen-mile drive comfortably. Soon after leaving Yale, two deer crossed the road a few yards in front of us. At the river, after being drawn over the ice in a hand-sleigh to the open water, we found the canoe awaiting us, and were paddled across by two Indians. It was no easy matter to climb the steep, slippery path on the other side; but that accomplished, we soon reached the inn, where as usual we received a hearty welcome.

On Wednesday morning at 7:30 we took our places in the sleigh, this time seated on the bottom, and without any hay for our backs. The bare boards seemed very hard, and every jolt shook us severely. The cold was intense, and we watched the sun rise, first over one mountain and then over another, longing for it to reach and warm us too a little. We had intended to get out and trust to our own legs going round the Bluff, thinking it safer, as one of our horses had lost a shoe. Our driver, however, never stopped, thinking that he could take us safely round. My heart seemed to stop beating as I felt the sleigh slid- ing, sliding, till one corner where I sat was off the road overhanging the river. The chain which forms a drag round one of the runners turned the hinder part of the sleigh outwards. Happily, the horses kept a firm hold of the ice, and we were soon on safer ground. The road round the Bluff is not more than fifteen feet above the level of the river, but it is directly below, and runs, as at all the bars, very swiftly. The road certainly was worse than when we came up, but on the whole we felt little disposed to quarrel with our jolting.

We reached Chilliwack about four o'clock, and found the place in great excitement over a "Social" that was to take place that night, and at which I had promised to sing. I was very tired, and it was kindly arranged that both my songs should be in the second part, so that we might remain quietly in the hotel during the first half.

Much to our relief, the *Gem* arrived that very evening. Ice had formed on the river during the last few cold nights to such an extent that there had been grave doubts whether she would be able to get up. We embarked about nine on Thursday morning, and were soon on our way down the river. There was much floating ice, and, for the protection of the boat, rough planks had been nailed on to the bows. The ice, however, made short work of these. Then they tried lashing two trees at a sharp angle before the bows, but the ice soon cut the lashings through. At Langley there is a small loop of the river, into which the captain tried to go to land the mails, but it was so blocked with ice that this was found to be impossible, and it was a difficult matter to get out again. It took a whole hour to get out where we had been but a few minutes getting in.

The *Gem* is not a boat in which one can feel much security. The ice here was but a few inches thick, while that we passed through last year in the Gulf of S. Lawrence was some feet, yet we were in more danger in the *Gem* than we had been in the *Sarmatian*. After getting out of our difficulty, and proceeding a short distance down the river, we encountered a fresh obstacle. The ice was closely packed across its entire width. The captain determined to try to get through, but soon found he must back out, and quickly, too, if the *Gem* was not to be fast shut in, as large masses of ice were coming down from above. When, after hard work, we were clear, it was decided to make fast to the shore and wait till the ice broke up. The ice had done some damage, which the crew set to work to repair. We were in sight of Maple Ridge, a settlement where we should have found comfortable quarters. We made for it, but, alas! There were no means of crossing the slough which lay between us and the wished-for goal, so we had to return to the steamboat, and spend the night on board. The weather had been warm all day, and rain seemed imminent. This captain and the engineer gave up to our use a small cabin on deck, their own sleeping quarters, and into this five persons were crowded. Sleep was out of the question, and at midnight (it was snowing hard), when looking out, I heard a curious roaring sound down the river. The captain came soon after, and explained that it was the tide coming up, lifting and breaking the ice, which by morning would be floated out to sea. He proved to be right, and at 6:30 on Friday morning we made a fresh start.

The engineer told us that during the night, finding that the boat was taking more water than he could account for, he took a light and went round to examine, and found that one of the main planks had been started by the ice, and that but for a coating of ice she would have filled still faster.

By 9 a.m. we were landed at Sapperton, heartily glad to be at home again, after a trip which, in spite of its roughness, had been on the whole thoroughly enjoyed.[35]

In 1885 Violet recorded her trip from Kamloops to the Columbia River. The journey began in May, and despite the early season, the forests were dry enough that fire was a definite hazard. They encountered fire on three separate occasions on this trip. Two occasions are described here, excerpted from the longer narrative.

On Friday, May 1st, we were up at 6 a.m., with a very large cargo on board [the steamboat *Peerless*], and a very rough crowd of passengers, numbering, Chinese included, nearly two hundred. The men were on their way up to work on different parts of the railway line. We spent a pleasant, lazy day, going slowly up the South Thompson river, often getting on the sand-bars—for the river was very low. Our progress was so slow that, instead of arriving at Eagle Pass [Landing, near today's Sicamous] at 10 p.m., it was six the following morning ere we arrived at that landing.

It was 9 a.m. before we were able to 'hitch up' our horses and drive off. The morning had been misty, and so we were unable to see much of the Lesser Shuswap Lake, on the shores of which we had been landed. The day was very warm, and the sun scorching, yet all around snow lay on the ground, quite thick in the more sheltered places. The trees all along the road were wonderful. The timber of British

Columbia is generally very fine, in some places extraordinarily large, but never had we seen anything to equal this amongst which we now were—cedars for the most part so tall and straight that the tops were scarcely visible. About seven o'clock, when still three miles from our destination, we were stopped at a camp with the news that it would be impossible for us to proceed at present, as forest fires were raging ahead, and the road was blocked with fallen trees. They were expecting every moment the return of a party who had been engaged all day in clearing the road. Soon we met the 'boss,' who told us the fire was very bad, but that there were only a few more trees to clear away, and that he would send out a fresh gang of men and get us through if possible. We put-to the ponies, and, following the men, came up to them whilst they were chopping out the two last trees. It was by no means pleasant waiting in the midst of such fire and smoke, one's eyes streaming with tears, yet unable to withdraw them [the eyes] from the falling trees, which were liable to come down at any moment. Against one large cedar we were especially warned to be on our guard, and whilst watching this, down fell another between ourselves and the choppers, not many yards from either of us. How those men worked! Englishmen have little idea how, under ordinary circumstances, Canadian axemen can chop, but when working, as they then were, with almost superhuman efforts, it was a sight requiring to be seen to be believed.

At last the road was clear, and the boss told the Bishop to whip the ponies "all he knew how," and gallop through. This he did, though at first it looked impossible, the bushes burning fiercely on either side, and the flames blowing right across the road, the dense smoke making everything else look dark. We did as we were told, and the ponies seeming fully to understand that this was a time for a special effort, galloped, and we, with our heads bent down, went through safely, the large cedar falling directly after....[36]

On the return journey they again contended with the frightening situation of forest fires.

We had intended to leave the Columbia in time to catch the Saturday's boat from Eagle Pass [Landing], as we were due in Kamloops on Sunday. But this was not possible. The road was blocked with fallen trees, and men could not be spared to clear them away, the house being by

View of Kamloops from the east, 1885.
PHOTOGRAPHER: THOMAS FAWCETT. B.C. ARCHIVES H-00249.

West end of Kamloops, 1887.
PHOTOGRAPHER: THOMAS FAWCETT. B.C. ARCHIVES A-03632.

no means out of danger. It was not, therefore, till midday on Sunday, after a morning service, that we said goodbye to our kind and hospitable hostess, and started, not knowing, indeed, how far we might be able to get without being stopped; for information had come that the fires were very bad along the whole road. For the first seven miles we had an escort with an axe, and very thankful we were for his help in unhitching the horses and getting the buckboard across two burnt-out culverts and some fallen trees.

We crossed the lakes without trouble, reaching Griffin Lake about 7:30, where we found a number of teams waiting to get over the road. After an all too short night's rest, we started at 6 am., hoping, oh! so heartily, that the road might be clear, knowing with satisfaction that when we had accomplished the first ten miles, we should afterwards have one, or perhaps two, teams ahead. We, therefore, hurried on, as, being only our two selves in the buckboard, company would be very desirable in getting over our difficulties.

Our hopes were, alas! futile. Hardly had we driven a mile before we found a tree fallen right across the road, with no possibility of getting round it, so we unhitched, and the Bishop chopped out the smaller branches. He then made the ponies jump over, and we proceeded to lift over the buckboard. Never had it seemed so heavy before, and, indeed, once or twice I felt almost hopeless. But time and perseverance accomplish most things, and so with this, though a number of bruises bore testimony that the task was by no means an easy one. Other logs we encountered, but were able to get round some, and we were fortunate in getting the help of men to get past others. The ten miles ended, we believed our troubles to have come to an end, and drove on with lighter hearts over the fresh wheel-tracks, but the first man we met informed us that the fires were so bad three miles further on that we should be stopped, and that a large bridge had been burnt during the night. This was not cheering; but thinking that where one team had gone another might follow, we proceeded, but were soon stopped by our friend, the overseer, who had conducted us through the first fire on our journey up. He recommended us to turn back, as we could not possibly get through until the next day. He said that not only was the bridge burnt, but the trees were falling so fast that it would be dangerous to go near where the repair party was already at work.

Still, we pushed on, for the steamboat was to leave the landing that evening. Reaching the fire, the Bishop alighted, leaving me in the buckboard while he walked on. After a long, anxious wait, I heard his voice calling me to come on, and he brought the welcome news that the road was clear to the bridge if we could drive through very hot fires, and that the men would try and lift over the buckboard. Well, we got through, I know not how, and reaching the bridge, found quite an assemblage; for besides the repair party, there were two teams, a band of wild cattle, and a loaded pack-train, waiting on the other side. It seemed a big gap over which to lift the buckboard, but many hands make light work, and to cross the bridge did not take a quarter of the time it had taken us to cross some of the trees. Before the steamer had been many minutes at the landing, we had taken leave of our friends, and retired to a fairly comfortable cabin....

Stagecoach at the summit of the Eagle Pass Wagon Road, ca. 1885. Note the charred trees, sign of a recent forest fire not unlike that encountered by Violet and her husband.
PHOTOGRAPHER: UNKNOWN. B.C. ARCHIVES I-30805.

After this our journey was uneventful, and we reached Kamloops in the afternoon of Saturday, with hearts full of thankfulness at having been safely brought through so many dangers.[37]

The Sillitoes did not reach parts of the East and West Kootenay area until 1890, when the Bishop decided to "spy out the land." The town of Nelson was just coming into existence, and silver and other mining ventures had begun to open up the area for settlement.

The C.P.R. took us as far as Revelstoke,—quite a change from the earlier method of travel! From Revelstoke a steamer took us down the Columbia, through the beautiful Arrow Lakes to Sproat. The rest of the journey was made riding over a very rough trail to Nelson.

At Sproat['s Landing, now Robson] we stayed at the Hotel Kootenay. The name calls up visions of comfort and luxury which were wholly without foundation. The house had been run up a few months earlier, and absolutely green lumber had been used, with the result that when the warm weather came the boards shrank, leaving gaps varying from half an inch to two inches between them. The privacy of the rooms was therefore nominal. From our bedroom we could look through into the next room, and through that into the room beyond, out into the passage and into the room opposite, and down through the floor into the dining-room, to see how the preparations for the next meal were getting on. Not that the meal had much interest, for dry crackers and cold water was the only thing I could manage, and we had to stay a whole day, as horses had to be procured for the ride to Nelson,—one of the roughest rides I ever experienced.

Arrived in Nelson, we found comfortable quarters in the Nelson House, the only house that was completed. There were others half built, and lots of canvas-roofed shacks and tents of every description. Nelson at that time was a typical Bret Harte mining camp, though these conditions did not last long. The lawless element, which had come from the other side of the line, soon drifted out when the men found that British law and order was to prevail. The Bishop arranged for the loan of a half-built store for the Sunday services, and we swept out and arranged this, laying planks between nail-kegs for seats. We had found three old friends in Nelson, who promised to help with the singing, and at 11 o'clock these three men, the Bishop and I were in the

Stagecoach on the road to Nelson, 1890s.
PHOTOGRAPHER: UNKNOWN. B.C. ARCHIVES A-02074.

store ready to begin, the rest of the congregation (all men) remaining outside. The Bishop went to the door and invited them in, but nothing came of it, and, after a second invitation had like results, the Bishop commenced the service. As soon, however as the singing began, in they all trooped and the store was filled. I think perhaps it was the most curious service I had ever attended, and there had been many that tried my gravity almost to the breaking point. During the sermon the men made remarks and criticisms, just as if it were a political meeting. These interruptions did not seem to worry the Bishop. Not so one of the younger parsons, who some time later was taking service in one of the camps, and, perhaps a little unwisely, with a gathering such as it was, used the regular prayer-book service. The prayer for the Queen passed without comment, but when the prayer for the Royal Family began a miner remarked, "Stop right there, parson; we don't mind praying for the old lady, but I'll be hanged if we'll pray for the rest of the lot." (I am afraid that perhaps the expressions used were somewhat stronger than I have quoted)....[38]

The hospitality of all those they met on the road is echoed in the records of Violet's contemporaries[39] and was no doubt due in large part to the importance of human contact in isolated settlements. Nevertheless, the situation, in many instances, of being the only white woman in a settlement of miners could be unsettling. Rarely did a woman travel unattended by male support. To become separated, even briefly, from the feeling of protection afforded by her husband was frightening. Even an experienced traveller such as Violet Sillitoe could quickly become insecure, as the following extract will illustrate.

In travelling about B.C. as we did every year, we met with the most wonderful hospitality. We could turn up quite unexpectedly at the most busy season of the year, or probably at other times equally inconvenient, but always the same smiling welcome was accorded; only once in all those years do I remember being turned away, probably for some good reason. I have no recollection now of what it was, but I do remember the sinking of heart I experienced, for it was late in the afternoon, the next stopping place being fifteen miles further on—a long stretch for tired horses, to say nothing of ourselves. By the time we reached our second destination it was quite dark. Our host came out to welcome us and then went with the Bishop to unharness and see after the comfort of our horses. This was a job my husband always attended to himself, and he did not leave until the horses were rubbed down and comfortably stabled; always the first thing in the morning

Spallumcheen, B.C., 1889. Group in front of Wood and Rabbet Store.
PHOTOGRAPHER: UNKNOWN. B.C. ARCHIVES A-06965.

Miners, Silver King Mine, Nelson, B.C., 1890s.
PHOTOGRAPHER: UNKNOWN. B.C. ARCHIVES A-02064.

View of Nelson, B.C., ca. 1893. Note charred trees on slope behind town.
PHOTOGRAPHER: NEELANDS. B.C. ARCHIVES A-03147.

Revelstoke, B.C., ca. 1889. East end of lower town, Columbia Hotel on the right.
PHOTOGRAPHER: UNKNOWN. B.C. ARCHIVES C-08525.

he was out again at the stables scraping the collars, greasing the axles and generally over-hauling the harness. This particular stopping place boasted of no women kind. I had been ushered into a large barroom, or at least what appeared to be one, with ten or twelve men lounging about. I was very tired, and, making for the nearest chair, felt a great inclination to weep. The real dangers of the road, so long as my husband was with me, were as nothing, but to be left unprotected in the company of so many unknown men was terrifying. It soon became evident that if I were frightened of the men they were equally so of me, for one by one they made their way out, and I was left absolutely alone. When our host returned, he asked if he could show me to my cabin, and at first I thought he must have been a seafaring man, but no; following the light of the lantern he carried, he ushered us into a one-room cabin with mud floor and just two beds, not another thing, and our host made many apologies to me for the absence of a looking-glass! After supper the men again gathered together, and the Bishop held a short service, and then, after I had retired, he stayed on awhile to have a smoke and talk with them.[40]

Bishop Sillitoe was enormously popular not only because of the force of his personality but also because he made little distinction in ministering to all classes and races of people in his diocese. He was committed to education for all and to this end established mission districts with schools for Indigenous people. Rather than focussing on their conversion to Christianity as an end in itself, Sillitoe was adamant that "the one thing they require to lift them above their present civilization [is], namely, simple but efficient secular education."[41] He and Violet actively supported the mission schools which he initiated within the diocese. Much time was spent meeting with Indigenous people, one-on-one, in attempts to convince them of the importance of education for their future livelihood. Sillitoe also founded a Chinese school in Vancouver, at a time when racial intolerance towards Chinese people was at its height.

Sillitoe's particular passion was found in music and he founded the New Westminster Choral Union in 1882. Violet also enjoyed music and loved to sing, as has been mentioned in previous extracts. She believed that this love of music played an important part in her husband's success.

Music was a great pleasure to all classes, and the Bishop always carried with him on his journeys a baritone concertina, a beautiful instrument, with tone like an organ, and with this he accompanied the singing at the services, and he also often played, and I sang during the evenings. It is funny, no doubt to think of a Bishop in his robes taking a service and playing a concertina, but that concertina opened doors that might otherwise have been forever closed, and people came to the services attracted by the music, and were perhaps reminded of things they had learned years before and had forgotten.[42]

Violet and her husband travelled through the diocese fairly consistently for over a decade. In 1892 the bishop's strength ebbed, and he never resumed those intense travelling days. In 1894, after two years of general weakness and illness, Bishop Sillitoe died in great pain from blood poisoning and kidney failure. Bright's Disease, as it was called, had not been correctly diagnosed until it reached an acute and untreatable stage. Violet was thus widowed at the relatively young age of 38. She lived on another 40 years, dying in Vancouver in 1937. She had no children, but her brother and sisters moved to British Columbia after her bereavement, and her family remained an important focus of her life. She remained active and committed to the church and worked unstintingly for the relief of prisoners of war during the First World War. In her will she bequeathed her "letters, letter-books, manuscripts and papers" to a sister, knowing that her records would be of interest and historical significance.

Violet came to British Columbia at the age of 24, having newly assumed important responsibilities as the wife and helpmate of the bishop. Sillitoe was 15 years older than his wife, and at the time of the marriage, had much experience in his profession and in travel. Considering her young age and inexperience with regard to setting up and running a household, her handling of the royal visit, which made her a society hostess at the age of 26, shows that she was a woman of much strength of character and resourcefulness. She was in a unique position because, despite her young years, she was a public figure and therefore under scrutiny. She did not bear children, so did not have that common link with other women her age as bonding through pregnancies, assisting with childbirth and child-rearing featured largely in their lives.

Acton and Violet Sillitoe, ca. 1879. Taken prior to
boarding the *Sarmatian*, en route for British Columbia.
PHOTOGRAPHER: WALERY. CITY OF VANCOUVER ARCHIVES PORT. P745.

The extraordinary amount of time travelling through the diocese necessarily meant that she relied on her husband for companionship, and indeed, as one incident illustrated, she relied heavily upon him for her sense of security. The immigrant society in the interior of B.C. was scattered along the Fraser and Thompson rivers, and on Okanagan Lake. Tiny pockets also existed in the Kootenay area. The Indigenous population was concentrated up the Fraser River—principally between Hope and Lytton—and on the Nicola and Thompson Rivers and the Okanagan and Kootenay Lakes. Travelling through the diocese, Violet would pass through pockets of existing settlement, and then through stretches where

Violet Sillitoe in the 1930s.
PHOTOGRAPHER: UNKNOWN. ARCHIVES OF THE ANGLICAN
DIOCESE OF NEW WESTMINSTER.

the land was largely depopulated. The distance between settlements and the infrequency of seeing other travellers could be disconcerting. In the event of an emergency, what would she do?

A benefit of travelling beyond the urban areas was that the pressures of society and the expectations of a bishop's wife became somewhat relaxed. She was free to act in her own fashion, not worried about society and its standards. In contrast to Kate Woods, whose overland journey stopped on each Sabbath for a day of rest, the Sillitoes spent Sundays in travel, anxious to reach the next stop. To Violet, this afforded a unique opportunity. In order to allow the Bishop to rest, she took over the horses. "On these days I used to drive as much as possible, so as to save the Bishop."[43] Learning to drive the buckboard was wise, as one emergency situation, when the Bishop was suffering from a carbuncle on his spine, required that she drive unaided from Quesnel to Yale.

Violet herself summarized her vagabond life with the Bishop, saying:

> We travelled in all sorts of ways,—riding, driving, canoeing, walking, working ourselves along the railway on a handcar, but this last was a rather anxious way of getting about. The line was a single one, and freight trains might and did travel at a high rate of speed, and meeting one rounding a sharp curve made it touch and go if we could remove ourselves and our hand-car in time, and it did not do to be caught on a bridge, either walking or by hand-car....
>
> These experiences about which I have tried to tell you lasted from 1880 until the time of my husband's death in 1894. The hardships and discomforts we endured were undoubtedly great, but they only made the comforts of home seem the greater from the contrast, and the joy of those years must always remain one of my most precious memories.[44]

NOTES

1 Violet E. Sillitoe, *Pioneer Days in British Columbia* (Vancouver: private publication, 1923), pp. 3–4.

2 See Roberta L. Bagshaw, *No Better Land* (Victoria: Sono Nis Press, 1996) and end-notes in chapter on Kate Woods for further details about the Hills.

3 *Pioneer Days*, p. 4.

4 Ibid., pp. 4–5.

5 Canada Census, 1881, quoted in Cole Harris, *The Resettlement of British Columbia* (Vancouver: University of British Columbia Press, 1996), pp. 138–9, 153, 294.

6 Ibid.

7 George Hills, diary, quoted in Bagshaw, *No Better Land*, p. 161.

8 William Ridley (1836–1911).

9 The diocese was some 160,000 square miles. Rev. Charles H. Mockridge, *The Bishops of the Church of England in Canada and Newfoundland* (Toronto: E.N.W. Brown, 1896), p. 322.

10 Some of Burdett-Coutts' philanthropic projects in the diocese have been noted in previous chapters.

11 Violet E. Sillitoe, *Early Days in British Columbia* (Vancouver: private publication, 1922), p. 10.

12 Charles R. Baskett was described in the 1879 *Columbia Mission Annual Report* Clergy List as the "Missionary at Hastings." See Frank A. Peake, *The Anglican Church in British Columbia* (Vancouver: Mitchell Press, 1959).

13 *Pioneer Days*, pp. 5–7.

14 *Early Days*, p. 4.

15 *Pioneer Days*, preface.

16 H.H. Gowan, *Church Work in British Columbia: Being a Memoir of the Episcopate of Acton Windeyer Sillitoe, First Bishop of New Westminster* (Condon: William Clowes and Sons, 1899).

17 *Mission Life* (London: Wells Gardner, Darton & Co., 1882–1892), *Columbia Mission Annual Reports* (London: Rivingtons, 1882–1892).

18 *Pioneer Days*, pp. 7–8.

19 Archdeacon Richard Small (1849–1909) was for many years resident at Lytton, administrator to the area bounded by Hope, Kamloops and Lillooet. Rev. Henry Edwardes worked under Small's direction.

20 *Pioneer Days*, pp. 18–19.

21 Rosa Kendal was enumerated in the 1881 Canada Census as Rosa Rendall, aged 25. She was the principal at Columbia College and lived with Archdeacon Woods and his family.

22 *Pioneer Days*, pp. 12–17.

23 Forbes Vernon and his brother Charles, formerly of the Lancashire Fusiliers, came to British Columbia and invested in land, establishing the Coldstream Ranch just outside the future town of Vernon. The brothers sold the ranch in 1891. See Patrick A. Dunae, *Gentlemen Emigrants: From the British Schools to the Canadian Frontier* (Vancouver: Douglas and McIntyre, 1981).

24 *Early Days*, pp. 12–13.

25 Ibid., pp. 14–16.

26 Ibid., pp. 16–17.

27 Ibid., pp. 17–18.

28 Gowan, p. 68.

29 Pakyst is Pukaist Creek, which flows southwest into the Thompson River, near the former CPR stop of Spatsum. Pukaist, or Pokeist, is a Nlaka'pamux word for "white rock." G.P.V. Akrigg and Helen B. Akrigg, *British Columbia Place Names* (Victoria: Sono Nis Press, 1988).

30 Chief William Meshell was an Indigenous interpreter who also assisted Archdeacon Small and Bishop Sillitoe in promoting the Church within the native community. Gowan, pp. 128, 162.

31 N'Chakup, variously spelled "Nyshakup," is possibly the Nesikep 6 Reserve, located on both banks of the Fraser River twelve miles south of Lillooet.

32 Gowan, pp. 180–184.

33 Oham'l is the name of a Sto'lö native village on the southern shore of the Fraser River near Chilliwack.

34 Rev. Robert Chesstyre Whiteway worked at the missions at Yale and Lytton; Rev. C. Blanchard, ordained as a priest in 1881, went to the Cariboo-Barkerville area.

35 Gowan, pp. 32–36.

36 Gowan, pp. 146–147.

37 Gowan, pp. 152–154.

38 *Early Days*, pp. 30–31.

39 See Sarah Crease's 1880 journal, kept on a trip to the Cariboo. She and her husband followed the Sillitoes by a day, northward along the Cariboo Wagon Road. Transcribed in Kathryn Bridge, *Henry & Self: An English Gentlewoman at the Edge of Empire* (Victoria: Sono Nis Press, 1996; Royal BC Museum, 2019).

40 *Pioneer Days*, pp. 19–20.

41 Acton Sillitoe, quoted in Gowan, p. 62.

42 *Early Days*, p. 32.

43 Ibid., p. 16.

44 Ibid., pp. 32–33.

Sources

SELECT MANUSCRIPT AND NEWSPAPER SOURCES

British Colonist (newspaper: 1858–1865), Victoria, British Columbia.

British Columbia Vital Statistics Agency. Death and marriage certificates. B.C. Archives.

Brown, Robert. Robert Brown Papers, correspondence outward 1865–1895, B.C. Archives.

Canada census records, 1881.

Crease and Lindley families. Crease Family Fonds, Correspondence, Diaries, Notebooks, Artworks, Photographs and Maps created and maintained by various family members, notably Sarah, Henry, Susan, Josephine and Mary Crease, ca. 1801–1968. B.C. Archives.

Daily Chronicle (newspaper: 1862–1866), Victoria, British Columbia.

Fawcett Family Fonds, Diaries, correspondence and memoirs. B.C. Archives.

Fellows, Arthur Jr. Arthur Fellows Papers. 1920s to 1930s, Bruce Castle Museum.

———. Correspondence outward. B.C. Archives.

Fellows, Caroline Frances. Correspondence outward, B.C. Archives.

Fellows, Eleanor C. The Brazen Horseman. Brighton: unpublished, typeset 1846. British Library.

Goodfellow, Florence. Memories of Pioneer Life in British Columbia. Typescript, 1929–1933, B.C. Archives.

Hazelton Queek (newspaper: 1880–1881), Hazelton: privately printed.

Mainland Guardian (newspaper), New Westminster, British Columbia.

New Westminster Times (newspaper: 1858–1865), New Westminster, British Columbia.

O'Reilly Family Fonds. Diaries, Correspondence, notebooks and other materials created and maintained by Peter, Caroline and Charlotte Kathleen O'Reilly. B.C. Archives.

Pringle, Alexander David. Correspondence. B.C. Archives.

Tomlinson, Alice. Wayside Log, journal kept April to July 1878. B.C. Archives.

Victoria Gazette (newspaper: 1858–1866), Victoria, British Columbia.

Woods, Helen Kate. Diary of a Journey, April 1880. B.C. Archives.

PUBLISHED SOURCES

Akrigg, G.P.V. and Helen B. *British Columbia Place Names*. Victoria: Sono Nis Press, 1988.

Bagshaw, Roberta L. *No Better Land: The 1860 Journals of the Anglican Colonial Bishop George Hills*. Victoria: Sono Nis Press, 1996.

Barman, Jean. *The West Beyond the West*. Toronto: University of Toronto Press, 1991.

Baskerville, Peter. *Beyond the Island: An Illustrated History of Victoria*. Burlington: Windsor Publications Ltd., 1986.

Blyth, Gladys Young. *Salmon Canneries, British Columbia North Coas*t. Lantzville: Oolichan Books, 1991.

Bridge, Kathryn. "Two Victorian Gentlewomen in the Colonies of Vancouver Island and British Columbia: Eleanor Hill Fellows and Sarah Lindley Crease." M.A. thesis, University of Victoria, 1984.

———. *Henry & Self: An English Gentlewoman at the Edge of Empire*. Victoria: Sono Nis Press, 1996; Royal BC Museum, 2019.

Duffus, Maureen. *Craigflower Country*. Victoria: self-published, 1993.

———. *A Most Unusual Colony*. Victoria: self-published, 1996.

Dunae, Patrick A. *Gentlemen Emigrants: From the British Public Schools to the Canadian Frontier*. Vancouver: Douglas and McIntyre, 1981.

Fawcett, Edgar. *Some Reminiscences of Old Victoria*. Toronto: W. Briggs, 1912.

Fellows, Eleanor C. "Nova Scotia's Cry for Home Rule." *The Nineteenth Century*. London: Kegan, Paul, Trenen and Co., 1886.

———. *Truth vs Fiction, re: The Chalmers' Claim*. London: R. Forder, 1892.

Forbes, Elizabeth. *Wild Roses at their Feet: Pioneer Women of Vancouver Island*. Vancouver: Evergreen Press Ltd., 1971.

Goodfellow, Florence. *Memories of Pioneer Life in British Columbia*. Kent Centennial Committee, 1958.

Gowan, H. H. *Church Work in British Columbia: Being a Memoir of the Episcopate of Acton Windeyer Sillitoe, First Bishop of New Westminster.* London: William Clowes and Sons, 1899.

Grove, Lyndon. *Pacific Pilgrims.* Vancouver: Fforbez Publications Ltd., 1979.

Harris, Cole, ed. *The Resettlement of British Columbia.* Vancouver: University of British Columbia Press, 1997.

Hendrickson, James Emil, ed. *Journals of the Colonial Legislatures of the Colonies of Vancouver Island and British Columbia, 1851–1871.* Victoria: Provincial Archives of British Columbia, 1980.

Lugrin, N. De B. *Pioneer Women of Vancouver Island 1843–1866.* Victoria: The Women's Canadian Club, 1928.

Macfie, Matthew. *Vancouver Island and British Columbia.* London: Longman, Green, 1865.

Mockridge, Charles H. *The Bishops of the Church of England in Canada and Newfoundland.* Toronto: F.N.W. Brown, 1896.

Murray, Peter. *The Devil and Mr. Duncan: A History of the Two Metlakatlas.* Victoria: Sono Nis Press, 1985.

Ormsby, Margaret A. *A Pioneer Gentlewoman in British Columbia: The Recollections of Susan Allison.* Vancouver: University of British Columbia Press, 1976.

Patenaude, Branwen C. *Trails to Gold.* Victoria: Horsdal and Schubart, 1995.

———. *Trails to Gold.* Vol. 2, *Roadhouses of the Cariboo.* Surrey: Heritage House, 1996.

Patterson, E. Palmer. *Mission on the Nass.* Waterloo: Eulachon Press, 1982.

Peake, Frank A. *The Anglican Church in British Columbia.* Vancouver: Mitchell Press, 1959.

Perry, Adele. "'I'm So Sick of the Faces of Men': Gender Imbalance, Race, Sexuality and Sociality in Nineteenth Century B.C." *B.C. Studies* Spring/Summer 1995.

Pritchard, Allan, ed. *Vancouver Island Letters of Edmund Hope Verney, 1862–65.* Vancouver: University British Columbia Press, 1996.

Rutherdale, Myra. "Revisiting Colonization through Gender: Anglican Missionary Women in the Pacific Northwest and the Arctic, 1860–1945." *B.C. Studies* Winter 1994.

Sillitoe, Violet E. "Summer Wanderings in New Westminster." Mission Life. London: Wells, Gardner, Darton & Co., 1881.

———. *Early Days in British Columbia.* Vancouver: private publication, 1922.

————. *Pioneer Days in British Columbia.* Vancouver: private publication, 1923.

Silverman, Elaine Leslau. "Writing Canadian Women's History, 1970–1982: An Historiographical Analysis." *Canadian Historical Review* 63 (1982).

Smyth, Eleanor C. *Sir Rowland Hill: The Story of the Great Reform.* London: Fisher Unwin Ltd., 1907.

————. *An Octogenarian's Reminiscences.* Letchworth: private publication, 1916.

————. *A Thirteenth Century Prophet and Some of His Contemporaries.* Bexhill on Sea: private publication, 1923.

————. *An Essay on Chaucer.* Bexhill on Sea: private publication, 1924.

————. *The Passing of the Penny Post.* London: private publication, 1981.

Stephen, Sir Leslie and Sir Sidney Lee, eds. *Dictionary of National Biography.* London: Oxford University Press, 1917.

Strong-Boag, Veronica. "Writing about Women." *Writing About Canada: A Handbook for Canadian Modern History*, ed. John Schultz. Scarborough: Prentice-Hall Canada, 1990.

Tomlinson, George. *Challenge the Wilderness.* Anchorage: Great Northwest Publishing and Distributing Co., 1991.

Wade, Mark S. *The Cariboo Road.* Victoria: The Haunted Bookshop, 1979.

Walden, Frederick E. "Social History of Victoria, British Columbia, 1858–1871." Essay for bachelor's degree, University of British Columbia, 1951.

Weir, Joan. *Catalysts and Watchdogs: B.C.'s Men of God: 1836–1871.* Victoria: Sono Nis Press, 1995.

Whitehead, Margaret, ed. *Now You Are My Brother: Missionaries in British Columbia.* Sound Heritage 34. Victoria: Provincial Archives of British Columbia, 1981.

The Williams' Official British Columbia Directory. Victoria: The Williams' B.C. Directory Co. Ltd., 1882.

Woods, J.J. *The Agassiz Harrison Valley: History and Development.* Kent: Kent Historical Committee, 1958.

Index

*Note: **Bold** indicates an illustration, a photograph, or information found in a caption.*

Agassiz, Connie, 22, 34, **41**

Agassiz, James Burwell, **14**, 15, 17, 34, 40

Agassiz, Jane Vandine Caroline, **14**, 15, 34, **35**, 37

Agassiz, Lewis Arthur (Arthur), **14**, 15, 17, 36, 40, **41**

Agassiz, Lewis Nunn: background, 13, 15, 43n2; in Florence Agassiz's writings, 40; income, 25; jobs in Yale and Hope, 20, 22, 24–25; leaves family to travel, 40; moves family to Agassiz farm, 26–27; pre-empts land, 25–26

Agassiz, Margaret Eliza Florence Askin (Florence), 11–46; about, 9; brother Arthur's accident, 36; domestic duties, 30; early experiences with Indigenous people, 18, 21, 27; early life, 13–15; education, 21, 31, 32–33, 36, 44n15; engagement and marriage, 37, 38, 40; family photograph, **41**; farm routine, 30, 34, 39; with first child, **12**; first winter and spring on Agassiz farm, 28–30; hair, 32–33; in her 80s, **42**; leaves school, 34; life in Yale, 22; mosquitoes, 30; mountainside fire, 32; relocates to Agassiz farm, 26–27; with siblings, **14**; with sister Jane, **35**; travels from London to the Cariboo, 15–20; travels from New Westminster

to Agassiz, 36–37; "wild adventure," 9, 13; writings, 40–42; as young woman, **39**

Agassiz, Mary Caroline (née Schram): childbirth, 22, 28, 34, 39; with family, **41**; in Florence Agassiz's writings, 39; illness, 34–35, 36; as mother and wife, 13; refuses to travel Cariboo Wagon Road, 20, 39; travels from London to the Cariboo, 15–16

Agassiz, Minnie, 22, **41**

Agassiz farm, 25, 26–27, 28, 30, 34

Alexandria Suspension bridge, 22–23, 44n19

Andrew, John Alexander, 138, **139**, **140**, 145n51

Angela College, **30**, 32, 45n30, 95, 142n8, 142n9

Anhaun [Cranberry River], 115, 117, 121

Ankihtlast, B.C., 97, 98, 131, 132, 141, 143n14

"Ankihtlast" (Woods), **132**

"Ankihtlast Mission" (Woods), **131**

"Aquilket River above bridge" (Woods), **135**

arch, Columbia Street, New Westminster, **163**

Arthur (Indigenous guide); arranges accommodations, 110; background,

105, 144n30; leaves expedition, 111, 112; sleigh, 104; as teacher, 111; travels over ice, 108

Barkerville, B.C., 165, 171
Baskett, Rev. Charles R., 153, 154, 155, 195n12
Big Slough, 27, 45n26
Birdcage Walk, 53, 54, 81, **82**, 88n38
"Bishop Sillitoe's cottage," **175**
Blanchard, Rev. C., 178, 196n34
Bob (friend of Mr. Nice), 106, 144n32
Boys' Collegiate School, 93–94
"bride ship," 5
Bristol, William Yale (Bill), 29, 36, 45n27, 177
British Columbia, as setting, 4–7
buckboard, travel by, 157, 161, 165, 170, 184, 194
Burdett-Coutts, Angela (Baroness), 44n12, 142n3, 142n8, 152–53, 195n10

camels, in British Columbia, 17, 43n5
Canadian Pacific Railway, 152, 156, 159
"Canōn on the Kishpiyouks River" (Woods), **133**
Canvas-town, 79–80
Careless, J.M.C., 10n1
Cariboo Wagon Road 19–20, 22, 23, 39, 44nn17–18, 152, 165–71, **167**, **168**, **169**
Catherine (Indigenous woman, possibly Catherine Ryan), 107–8, 144n34
Chapman's Bar Bluff, **167**
Charles, Mabel, 44n13
Charles, Mary Ann (née Birnie), 21, 37
Charles, William, 21, 44n13
childbirth, 22, 28, 34, 39, 191
China Bar Bluff, **168**
Chinese immigrants: gold rush, 87n22,

155; growing population, 155; intolerance toward, 190; as miners, 21, 112, 145n38; poll (head) tax, 74–75; railway workers, 180; as servants, 73–74, 157, 160
Church Missionary Society, 97, 99
Church of England, in B.C., 151
Cole Island (powder-magazine islet), 65, 88n34
colonialism: attitudes to Indigenous people, 55, 87n23; British attitude toward colonies, 5–6; class, 2, 5, 25; communication among white communities, 137; Eleanor Fellows on colonists' greed for Indigenous land, 72; female strength, 1; flexibility required by, 3; hierarchy of nationality, 80, 155; premise of, 5
Columbia College, 159, 196n21
Crease, Sarah, 80, 88n40, 197n39
Croasdaile, Henry,105, 144n28

daguerreotypes, 70, 88n37
Dewdney Trail, 44n16
Douglas, James, 15, 43n3, 53
Dufferin, Lord and Lady, 36, 37–38

Eagle Pass Wagon Road, **184**
Early Days in British Columbia (Sillitoe), 156
education: of colonist children, 21, 25, 39; of Eleanor Fellows, 49; of Florence Agassiz, 21, 31, 32–33, 36, 44n15; of Helen Kate Woods, 95, 142n9; of Indigenous peoples, 190
Edwardes, Rev. Henry, 158, 195n19
Emory's Bar, 18
Esquimalt Harbour, 5, 33, 54, 58, **61**, **63**, **72**, 95
An Essay on Chaucer (Fellows), 85

eulachen (oolichan), **102**, **103**, 105
"Eve's Granddaughter," 84, 86n19,
    90n67

Fellows, Alfred, 50, 89n60
Fellows, Arthur, 49–50, 53–54, 76, 77, 81,
    82, 84, 90n65
Fellows, Eleanor Caroline, 47–90; about,
    8, 49; on Chinese labourers, 73–75; on
    colonists' greed for Indigenous land,
    72; death, 85; describes Canvas-town,
    79–80; education, 49; "Eve's Grand-
    daughter," 84, 86n19, 90n67; family
    photographs, 80–84, **82**, **83**, 89nn59–
    61; fire at Thetis Cottage, 65; first
    children borne by, 54; friendships,
    78–80; and Indigenous peoples,
    56–58, 65–72, 73; on Indigenous work
    and work ethic, 65–67; intellectual
    influences, 77; leaves B.C., 84, 89n63;
    letters, **61**, 75, 88n43; marriage, 49–50,
    86n4; musical talents, 49, 75–76; on
    "noble savage," 65; publishes *An
    Octogenarian's Reminiscences*, 54–55,
    84; rats, 61–63; religious observance,
    77–78; shot at, 70–71; sketches, **57**, **61**,
    63, **64**, **66**; sociable with other
    immigrants, 80; social justice, 51, 55;
    story of "beggar," 67–69; story of John,
    66–67; story of Lucy, 69, 70, 88n35;
    Thetis Cottage, 54, 58–61, **60**, **61**, **66**,
    72, 81, 82, **83**, 87n31; time in France,
    49; travels from England to British
    Columbia, 50–53; viewed by peers,
    76–77, 81; writings, 55, 84–85,
    86n18–19; as young woman, **48**
Fellows, Frank, 50
Fellows, Louisa (née Morgan), 50, 89n60
Finlaison, Charles Stubbert, 17, 43n6
forest fires, 170, 180, 181–85, **184**, **189**
Fort Victoria, 4, 88n38

Fraser River, 18, 50, **167**, **168**, **170**, 175, 176
"the Frenchman's" (roadhouse), 23, 45n20
frontier: 3, 6–7, 10n1
frontier women: childbirth, 22, 28, 34, 39,
    191; excitement as characteristic, 7;
    and Indigenous people, 6, 55–56, 58,
    73; records of, 1–2, 7–8, 75; as
    trailblazers, 4; travel, 187–89; Violet
    Sillitoe on, 168–69

Garbally, 95, **96**, 97, 138
Gitxsan people, 97
Glennie, Mrs., 31, 44n15
Glennie, Thomas, 21, 44n15
gold rush: Cariboo, 4, 13, 54, 74, 78–79,
    165; Chinese immigrants, 87n22, 155;
    Fraser River, 4, 50; and Lewis Nunn
    Agassiz, 15
Goodfellow, John, 38, **39**
grease trails, 98, 99, **133**
Greenville, B.C., **108**
"Group of Indian Curiosities" (Fellows),
    64

Hankin, Margaret (née McCauley), 131,
    145n43
Hazelton Queek, **137**, 137–38
H.B.C. Brigade Trail, 44n16
head tax (poll tax), 74
Heat-ckq (Sansanah): background, 105–6;
    crossing ice by sleigh, 104; hunts, 126,
    127; and Kate Woods's watch, 128;
    prepares "ish," 121–22; pull sleigh,
    112; as teacher, 113; tows canoe, 110
Hill, Rowland, 49, 55, 75, 76, 77, 88n42
Hills, George, 93, 94, 142n3, 142n8, 150,
    151, **166**
Hope, 20–21, 25, 26, 31, 44n14, 44n16,
    166
Hotel Kootenay, 185
"A House in the Woods" (Fellows), 58–72

immigrant population, 5, 144n28, 151
"Indian Bridge over Aquilket [Hagwilget]
River" (Woods), **134**
"An Indian Gathering at Hope, B.C.," **166**
"The Indian Mode of Rocking the Baby"
(Fellows), **63**
"Indian Village, Victoria Harbor, and
Plan of Hut" (Fellows), **57**
Indigenous people: as childcare givers for
colonists, 34; Christianity, 151; City of
Victoria by-law, 56; colonists' attitude
towards, 3, 6, 55–56, 87n23; education
of, 190; Eleanor Fellows on, 56–58,
65–72; "Group of Indian Curiosities"
(Fellows), **64**; as guides, 26, 27, 99,
104, 105–6, 111, 120, 143n23,
144nn30–31; housing, 21, 56–58, **57**,
110; "An Indian Gathering at Hope,
B.C.," **166**; "Indian Missions," 153;
"The Indian Mode of Rocking the
Baby" (Fellows), **63**; as interpreters,
196n30; and Kate Woods, 122, 141; as
labourers, 21, 27, 29, 66–67, 70,
88n40; liquor law, 174; living at
Ankihtlast mission, 98; Meshell,
William (Chief), 172, 196n30;
population numbers, 6, 141, 151, 193;
"Very like my Lucy" ("Tu-te-ma"), **68**;
view of Indigenous village, Victoria
Harbour, 1870s, **59**; and Violet Sillitoe,
155. *See also* Arthur (Indigenous
guide); Heat-ckq (Sansanah); Liggy
You-en ; Yack'o dades (Dades)
isolation, of settlers, 9, 98, 141, 168
Isthmus of Panama, 15, 50, 51, 94, 149

Jamieson (steamer captain), 17, 43n7

Kamloops, B.C., 17, 180, **182**
Keekwillie holes, 21
Kendal, Rosa, 159, 196n21

Kincolith, B.C., 97, 98, 99, **100**, 101, **102**,
103
Kit-lak-da-mich [Gitlakdamiks], 111
"Kitselass Canon" (Woods), **136**

landscape, 6–7
Landvoight, George and Mary, 21, 25,
44n14
Leigh, James Matthews, 86n2
Liggy You-en: background, 106, 144n31;
carries pack, 112; crossing ice by
sleigh, 104; falls on snowshoes, 127;
familiarity with trail, 121, 124, 145n41;
gives food, 121; hunts, 116, 126; tows
canoe, 110; travels over ice, 108
"Luandalahau River…Indian bridge…,"
(Woods), **117**
Lytton, B.C., **173**

Mabel Lake, 44n13
Maple Bank, 63, 87n33
Martineau, Harriet, 77
measles, on ship, 16
*Memories of Pioneer Life in British
Columbia* (Agassiz), 9, 13, 30, 41, 42,
43n1
Meshell, Chief William, 172, 196n30
"metropolitan thesis," 10n1
mining: around Nelson, 185; Miners,
Silver King Mine, **188**; Violet Sillitoe
describes, 171. *See also* gold rush
Mission House, 151, 178
Moresby, Annie, 43n10
mosquitoes, 18, 30
Mount St. Angela, 142n8. *See also* Angela
College
Murderer's Bar Bluff, 176

Nass River, **102**, 114, **115**, 115–16,
143–44n25
N'chakup Camp, 174–76, 196n31

"Near Salmon House, Anhaun River, April 22, 1880" (Woods), **118**

Nelson, B.C., 185–87, **186, 187, 189**

New Westminster, B.C., 36, 151, **152, 163**

Nice, John Byron, 105, 106, 144n27

Nisg̱a'a people, 97

"Nova Scotia's Cry for Home Rule" (Fellows), 55, 84

An Octogenarian's Reminiscences (Fellows), 8, 54–55, 58, 75, 78, 84

Oham'l (village), 177, 196n33

oolichan (eulachon), **102, 103,** 105

Oppenheimer, Charles and Harriet, 22, 44n17

Oppenheimers' store, 24

"Oregon question," 59–60

O'Reilly, Caroline, 80

pack horses nearing the Groundhog Summit, **125**

Pakyst (Pukaist Creek), 172, 196n29

The Passing of the Penny Post (Fellows), 85

Pemberton, Miss, 32, 45n30

photo albums, compiled by British Columbians, 80–81

Pioneer Days in British Columbia (Sillitoe), 156

poll tax (head tax), 74

powder-magazine islet (Cole Island), 65, 88n34

pre-emption of land, 25, 44n15, 45n24

Princess Louise (royal visit), 159, 160, 161

Pringle, Rev. A.D., 20, 25, 26, 43n11, 45n24

Pringle, Marie Louisa, 20, 22, 25, 43n11

Pukaist Creek (Pakyst), 172, 196n29

pumas, 63, 87n32

ratio, of men to women, 75, 168–69

rats, 61–63

records, created by women, 1, 2, 7–8, 75

relationships, marital, 3

remittances, importance of, 25

Revelstoke, B.C., **189**

Ridley (bishop), **137,** 138, 152

Roseberry Farm, 132, **135**

royal visit, Violet Sillitoe's account of, 159–62, 191

salmon cannery, **102,** 144n28

salmon fishing, **118,** 119

Sanders, Edward Howard, 20, 43n10

Sansanah. *See* Heat-ckq (Sansanah)

Sapperton, B.C., 153, 180

Schutt, Henry, 99, 103, 143n22, 144n34

"shint" (word for summer), 128

Sillitoe, Bishop Acton Windeyer: age at time of marriage, 191; biography of, 156; "Bishop Sillitoe's cottage," **175;** care of horses, 187–88; and Chinese population, 155; death, 191; diocese, 151; on education of Indigenous peoples, 190; "An Indian Gathering at Hope, B.C.," **166;** musical interests, 190–91; ordained bishop, 149, 152; responsibilities, 153; service in barn, 165; with Violet Sillitoe, **192;** visits Cariboo mining district, 165, 167–68

Sillitoe, Violet Emily, 147–97; about, 8; accommodation in Charles Baskett's house, 154; age at time of marriage, 191; on being a woman among men, 190; as buckboard driver, 194; on Chinese servant, 157, 160; describes camp life, 172–76; describes mining, 171; dogs, 157, 160; first months in B.C., 153–54; forest fires, 170, 181–85, **184;** horse "Punch," 161–62; with husband, **148, 192**; "An Indian Gathering at Hope, B.C.," **166**; and Indigenous people, 155; on law in Nelson mining camp, 185; letters, 156, 162, 171; on lives of women settlers, 168–69; on monotony of travel, 169–70; moves to own house, 155; musical interests, 190–91; as older woman, **193**; publishes *Early Days in British Columbia* and *Pioneer Days in British Columbia*, 156; on rattlesnake bite and remedy, 174; religious observances, 165, 167, 168, 172, 173, 174, 185–87; responsibilities as bishop's wife, 153, 155–56, 191; royal visit, 159–62, 191; significance of childlessness, 191; St. Mary's Mount, 153, 157–58, **158**, 159; story of sick child, 175–76; time at N'chakup Camp, 174–76; time in Lytton, **173**, 173–74; on travels, 194; travels Cariboo Wagon Road, 165–71; travels from England to B.C., 149–50; travels from Kamloops to Columbia River and back, 180–85; travels to interior, 162–65; travels to Nelson, 185–87; widowhood, 191; on winter travel, 176–80

Silver King Mine, **188**

Sir Rowland Hill: The Story of The Great Reform (Fellows), 85

"Skeena Forks at Hazelton" (Woods), **134**

sleigh, travel by, 104, 106–9, 177–78

Small, Rev. Richard, 158, 195n19

snowshoes, travel by, 112–13, 120, **122**, 122–23, 124, 127, 128

Society for the Propagation of the Gospel, 152

Songish (Songhees band), 72, 88n38

Spallumcheen, B.C., **188**

Spatsum station, 172, 173

St. Mary's Mount, 153, 157–58, **158**, 159

stagecoach, travel by, 166–67, **184, 186**

Stallschmidt family, 33, 45n31

steamer: carries buckboard and horses, 165; fuel, 18; *Gem*, 179–80; *Idaho*, 150; *Otter*, **101**; *Peerless*, 180; shipboard conditions, 51–52, 55, 149–50; travel by, 31–32, 50–51, 94, 101, 165, 184; *Yale*, 17, 18

Thetis Cottage, 54, 58–61, **60, 61, 66, 72,** 81, 82, **83,** 87n31

A Thirteenth Century Prophet and Some of His Contemporaries (Fellows), 85

"Three Mile Canon on the Fraser River," **170**

Tomlinson, Alice (née Woods), 97–99, **100,** 131, 143n15

Tomlinson, Robert, 97, 98, **100,** 111, 131, 132

Trutch, John, 22, 44n18

Trutch, Joseph, 22, 44n18, 44n19

Trutch, Julia, 80

Truth vs Fiction re: The Chalmer's Claim (Fellows), 84–85

Tsimshian people, 97

Turner, Frederick Jackson, 10n1

"Tu-te-ma" ("Very like my Lucy"), **68,** 88n35

Tynemouth (bride ship), 5

"Vale of Ankihtlast, from Mission House" (Woods), **136**

Vernon, B.C., 163, **164**

Vernon, Charles, 196n23

Vernon, Forbes, 163, 165, 196n23

"Very like my Lucy" ("Tu-te-ma"), **68,** 88n35

Victoria: described by Eleanor Fellows, 53; growth, 50, 72, 88n38; and religious intolerance, 77; social scene, 33, 37–38, 41, 43n3; view of, 1860, **53**
view from the Bishop's House at New Westminster, 1880s, **152**
"View in Esquimalt Harbor, looking West" (Fellows), **66**
"View in Esquimault Harbor, looking South," 1866 (Fellows), **61**
view of Indigenous village, Victoria Harbour, 1870s, **59**
"View of Victoria, Vancouver Island, 1860," **53**

wages, 26, 29
Whiteway, Robert Chesstyre, 178, 196n34
Whymper, Frederick, 81, **82**
Williams Lake, 15
wolves, 29, 63
women. *See* frontier women
Wood and Rabbet Store, **188**
Woods (Archdeacon), 38, 150, 196n21
Woods, Anne, 93, 142n1
Woods, Charles T., 93, 142n4, 143n15
Woods, Edward: arrival at Ankihtlast, 131; carries Kate Woods's pack, 112; on conserving provisions, 124; at ease, 110–11; on graves at salmon house, 120; journal, 143n25; marriage, 143n18; on mountain, 121; snowshoes, 123; "spoils" Kate Woods, 116; trail finding, 113; on travel by canoe, 110; travels to Ankihtlast, 97; weather readings, 138
Woods, Emily Henrietta, 93, 94, 95
Woods, Helen Kate, 91–145; about, 9, 93; attitude towards wilderness travel, 99; canoe travel on Nass River, 109–10; care of clothing and snowshoes in

camp, 122–23; as a child, **96**; chocolate, 127–28, 145n42; on conserving provisions, 123–24, 128; on crew, 105–6; crosses ice with sleigh, 104, 106–9; crossing bad ice, 115–16, 128; describes campfire, 113; describes graves at salmon house, 119–20; describes Nass River, 114; describes salmon fishing, **118**, 119; education, 95, 142n9; first camping-out experience, 109; Garbally, 95, **96**; *Hazelton Queek*, **137**–38; with husband and children, **140**; and Indigenous people, 122, 141; journal, scrapbooks, sketches, 99, **109**, **115**, **117**, **118**, **122**, **131**, **132–36**, 141, 143–44n25; at Kit-lak-da-mich [Gitlakdamiks], 111–12; leaves Ireland for Victoria, 93–95; marriage and widowhood, 138; "Mi" and "ish," 120, 121–22, 127, 145n40; on moccasins, 119; motive for trip to Ankihtlast, 99, 143n20; on proverbs, 117; reaches Ankihtlast, 131; religious observances, 111, 113–14; on snowshoe technique, 127; stay at Ankihtlast, 131–32, 141; stays with Indigenous family, 110–11; story of sleigh with sail, 107; travel by snowshoe along trail, 112–13; on travelling difficult trail, 120–21; travels to Ankihtlast, 97, 98, 99–131; treks through water, 130–31; watch, 128; as a young woman, **92**
Woods, Maria (née Kingsmill), 142n4
Woods, Richard, 93, 97, 142n1

Yack'o dades (Dades), 111, 112, 115, 121, 126–27
Yale, B.C., 18, 19, 20, 24, **164**, **169**